"This is an extraordinary, profound, poignant and true story, brilliantly and fascinatingly told. Human and animal relationships are complex and, when they involve captive wild animals, troubling to say the least. Even when, as we find here, there is deep mutual affection. In such an unnatural situation there can rarely be a 'happy ending.' I have almost never read a book which I longed to read again, as soon as I had turned the last page. Such is the subtlety, sensitivity and skill of Grant Hayter-Menzies' storytelling."
—Virginia McKenna, actor, author and co-founder of the Born Free Foundation

"Meticulously researched but also indulging an unapologetic and compelling stream of authorial speculation, this imaginative biography depicts two figures from two different species whose relationship, if imperfect, was fascinating and consummately intimate. *Woo, the Monkey Who Inspired Emily Carr* will certainly provoke reflections about our own animal companions: how we live with them, how they live with us."
—Randy Malamud, author of *Poetic Animals and Animal Souls* and *Reading Zoos*

"Grant Hayter-Menzies is an accomplished historian and writer, and *Woo, the Monkey Who Inspired Emily Carr* brings a unique perspective to the wide shelf of books regarding Emily Carr... The author's profound sympathy for all animals leads him to careful research into zoos, the trade in animals, animal behaviour and the long relationship between the legendary Canadian artist and the 'human-imprinted primate' who shared fifteen years with her. At once serious and fanciful, this is art history with a difference."
—Robert Amos, artist and former art writer for Victoria's *Times Colonist*

"Truthful and tender, a meticulously researched and fine reflection on the connection between art and animals."
—Anny Scoones, author of *Island Home*

Woo, the Monkey Who Inspired Emily Carr

GRANT HAYTER-MENZIES

with a foreword by Anita Kunz, OC

and an introduction by Andrew Westoll

WOO, THE MONKEY WHO INSPIRED EMILY CARR

→ A BIOGRAPHY ←

Douglas & McIntyre

1 2 3 4 5 — 23 22 21 20 19

Douglas and McIntyre (2013) Ltd.
P.O. Box 219, Madeira Park, BC, V0N 2H0
www.douglas-mcintyre.com

Edited by Derek Fairbridge
Indexed by Rebecca Pruitt MacKenney
Cover design by Anna Comfort O'Keeffe
Text design by Carleton Wilson
Printed and bound in Canada

Text is printed on 100% recycled paper

Canada

Conseil des Arts
du Canada

Douglas and McIntyre (2013) Ltd. acknowledges the support of the Canada Council for the Arts, which last year invested $153 million to bring the arts to Canadians throughout the country.

Nous remercions le Conseil des arts du Canada de son soutien. L'an dernier, le Conseil a investi 153 millions de dollars pour mettre de l'art dans la vie des Canadiennes et des Canadiens de tout le pays.

We also gratefully acknowledge financial support from the Government of Canada and from the Province of British Columbia through the BC Arts Council and the Book Publishing Tax Credit.

LIBRARY AND ARCHIVES CANADA CATALOGUING IN PUBLICATION

Hayter-Menzies, Grant, 1964-, author
Woo, the monkey who inspired Emily Carr : a biography / Grant Hayter-Menzies.

Includes bibliographical references and index.
Issued in print and electronic formats.
ISBN 978-1-77162-214-1 (softcover).--ISBN 978-1-77162-215-8 (HTML)

1. Woo (Monkey). 2. Carr, Emily, 1871-1945.
3. Monkeys--British Columbia--Biography. 4. Human-animal relationships. I. Title.

QL737.P93H39 2018 599.8'20929 C2018-906170-7
C2018-906171-

In honour of all the animals of Stanley Park Zoo and the Children's Farmyard (1888–2011).

❋

With thanks to those devoting their lives to saving and honouring the lives of our animal sisters and brothers.

❋

With love to Rudi and Freddie.

❋

In memory of Sweet Pea and of George.

CONTENTS

We went to the animal fair.
The birds and the beasts were there.
The big baboon, by the light of the moon,
was combing his auburn hair.

You ought to have seen the monk.
He jumped on the elephant's trunk.
The elephant sneezed and fell on his knees,
and what became of the monk,
the monk, the monk?

—Nursery rhyme

FOREWORD

Have you ever watched a monkey at play? Have you ever looked one in the eye and held his or her gaze? Have you ever communicated with one on any level? If you have, you will have experienced a kind of recognition, a sense of kinship. A profound connection based on a curious kind of shared knowing. In fact, we share a staggering amount of similar genetic material with these extraordinary creatures. And yet for some bizarre reason we are still legally allowed to "own" them in this culture. That concept in itself tells us how far we need to evolve if we are ever to become fully compassionate stewards of our increasingly fragile planet.

In my work as an artist I have for the past few years utilized images of monkeys as metaphors, as examples of how we as a species behave. In fact, I've often thought that we could explain a lot about human behaviour if we would only acknowledge the similar traits we share with wild simians—things like tribalism, politics (yes, politics), our inexplicable aggression even while we tell ourselves we are so special and unique, even our concepts of sex and falling in love.

And I'm not the only female artist who has been drawn to primates. Frida Kahlo included several of her monkeys as subjects in her paintings. And of course, the great painter Emily Carr and her monkey, Woo, who appears in two Carr paintings and numerous sketches, and is the subject of this book.

This passion for animals is something I'm all too familiar with. But sadly, what ends up happening to many of these remarkable pets is a later life of alienation and confusion that often ends in tragedy. The vast majority of primate pets or medical subjects are euthanized and only a few end up in the rare sanctuaries.

When I became aware of Story Book Farm Primate Sanctuary in Sunderland, Ontario (the only sanctuary for monkeys anywhere in Canada), and visited for the first time, I felt a sense of calling, a place where I could try to contribute in a meaningful way. I also felt a sense of injustice and urgency. Almost all of the residents there have sad histories but are now living out their lives in comfort and safety. I'm thrilled that proceeds from the sale of this book will go toward helping the sanctuary. And I'm so thrilled that such a wonderful writer has told this fascinating story of Emily Carr, an artist who was for far too long overlooked, and her beloved friend and muse Woo.

—Anita Kunz, OC

INTRODUCTION

I once knew a pet monkey. She was a brown capuchin named Amy, and she lived with a chain around her waist at the side of my friend Ganesh's house in Paramaribo, Suriname. Whenever my colleagues and I would come into the city from the jungle, where we were employed by the University of Florida as wild monkey researchers, we would visit Ganesh and Amy, and without fail these visits would elicit a peculiar sensation for us, a feeling we couldn't put our fingers on at the time but which in retrospect can only be described as confusion.

Our day jobs involved chasing troops of brown capuchin monkeys through the rainforest, and out in the bush we would never dream of attempting to physically touch, let alone play with, one of our study subjects. But now here we were, roughhousing with a young female capuchin, letting her climb all over our bodies, letting her groom our hair and skin as we returned the favour, feeling her tail tighten around our necks whenever a passing car would backfire or a random firework would go off. We loved Amy, but we hated seeing her chained to a wall. As for Ganesh, he hated the rainforest but worked as a cook for tourists in the jungle, and he loved Amy too.

From the Pharaohs' menageries of ancient Egypt, to the royal menageries of Europe in the Middle Ages, to the rise of the municipal zoo in the Victorian period, to the roadside zoos now dotted across the North American countryside, humans throughout history have kept wild animals in captivity, and for a myriad of reasons. To demonstrate and bolster their power and influence. To generate prestige for their families. As a symbol of their essential freedom as citizens. To pay the bills.

There is even an argument that suggests our inclination to cage the wild is a perversion of our love for it. In 1984, the biologist E.O. Wilson coined the term *biophilia,* the essential human affinity for all living things. We have a love for nature in our bones, in other words, so why not bring it into our homes?

Grant Hayter-Menzies, in this fascinating and beautifully written account of Emily Carr's relationship with her pet monkey, Woo, puts forth an entirely new thesis on this proclivity of ours to tame the exotic. Perhaps for some, proximity to the wild can unleash something profound in us, something previously inaccessible, undisclosed and certainly untamed.

"Animals were the fulcrum of Carr's greatness," writes Hayter-Menzies. And if the author is right when he suggests that "the motivating force behind art" is the expression of love, then how could Carr's affection for animals not factor into her masterpieces? From early childhood, Carr had "an ineluctable need to hold wild things." In her journals, the artist writes about belonging to Mother Earth, and how much she looked forward to settling down into nature's lasting embrace when she finally passed on.

And yet Carr was desperately frightened of monkeys. Hayter-Menzies activates this curious fact to suggest, compellingly, that Woo's presence in Carr's life was essential to her facing an unconscious fear of the true wild. In so doing, Woo becomes a vital spark to her creativity, and to the period of work that ultimately transformed Emily Carr into a Canadian icon.

Never far from the surface of this account is Hayter-Menzies's outrage as an animal advocate. The reader will appreciate the depth of his posthumous concern for Woo, how the monkey remains at the heart of the story throughout. (My favourite example: the author wonders if Carr's famous expeditions into nature were as rejuvenating for the chained-up Woo as they were for the artist herself.)

But Hayter-Menzies knows that it doesn't help to just look back in anger. Instead, if any of us hope to contribute to the monumental shift underway in our culture's response to animals, it can help to put aside our contemporary positions for a moment and examine some of history's most compelling human-animal bonds via the power of storytelling. This is how we can dig up the seeds of our fraught relationship with the natural world and replant them in renewed, more enlightened soils.

When I returned to Suriname five years later, one of the first things I did upon arriving in Paramaribo was inquire into the whereabouts of my old friend Ganesh. I quickly learned that he had moved into a larger home in the south of town, and as I pulled up to the house and took in the fact of its backyard, a jolt of excitement coursed through me. I didn't call out for my friend or knock on the front door. Instead, I snuck around back.

And there she was. Amy, now a beautiful sub-adult capuchin, sitting quietly in the lower branches of a magnificent fruit tree. When she saw me, she squealed and leaped up to a higher branch, and that's when I saw the chain was still around her waist but that it was longer now, long enough for her to reach the crown of her arboreal home and even browse among the fallen fruits and flowers on the ground below. Amy didn't recognize me, and that was a squeal of alarm, not delight. But in ten minutes she was back on my shoulders and grooming the hair on my head, her tail wrapped softly around my neck.

I don't know why Ganesh bought Amy. Was he after power, or prestige, or some inclination of personal freedom? I don't think so. Was he purposefully subjugating Amy for the sake of his ego? I doubt it. Had he rescued her from an unscrupulous dealer? No. But he loved her, I know that. Like the rest of us, Ganesh had a complicated relationship with the wild—he was the bush-cook who hated the bush—so why wouldn't this complication follow him home?

Hayter-Menzies's thesis about Emily Carr and Woo cuts to the heart of the whole enterprise. Maybe inspiration *is* the opportunity to face down our fears, and this is the essential seed of our obsession with the wild. Maybe the modern rise of exotic pet ownership across the West reflects not love for the wild per se, but a love for how the wild can make us think differently, feel more intensely and, in that rare case, create with abandon. Perhaps nature will always be our muse, no matter how deeply we mistreat her.

—Andrew Westoll

PROLOGUE

Named for Lord Stanley of Preston, sixteenth Earl of Derby, at its dedication in 1888, the 1001 acres of Stanley Park, which we now know as a beloved remnant of primeval Pacific Northwest rainforest held in the concrete embrace of Vancouver, had been exploited early for its resources by the growing city: its massive trees were logged right up till 1885.

For years the park also served as the site of a curious public menagerie, established informally in 1888, known as the Stanley Park Zoo. Maps from the early twentieth century mark quadrants of the park devoted to penned displays of buffalo, deer and goats. In the enclosures and pits and cages could be seen, over time, bears, birds, a seal, even kangaroos. As late as 1997, polar bears lived in a pit of stylized concrete slabs, a sort of Bauhaus concept of the North Pole.[1] The last bear, Tuk, paced his pit until death claimed him, and the entire concession was closed. Tuk, at least, had a quiet if prolonged end. Not so for the Chilean flamingos killed in 1992 by a suburban high school dropout who broke into their cage and beat the birds to death to prove to his friends how tough he was.[2]

Even without this grisly incident, however, the zoo's days were numbered. Right around the time of the flamingo killings, the Vancouver Park Board responded to public criticism of the zoo and the conditions in which animals were kept by coming up with an expensive interpretation and wildlife plan, the objective of which was to modernize the facilities and, by so doing, mollify censure. When this, too, rubbed Vancouverites the wrong way, a citywide referendum was called in November 1993. Consensus was clear:

close the zoo. (The petting zoo was also closed, albeit not for more than a dozen years.)[3]

Visiting Stanley Park today, you'll find little evidence that this zoo existed, apart from the stained and haunted polar bear pit, and the Vancouver Aquarium, which as of this writing has, like the zoo with its "exhibits," assented to public pressure to stop holding cetaceans in captivity.

Stanley Park Zoo is as dead as the animals who once lived there. But certain places, like certain people, leave behind them an indefinable, indelible mark. Sometimes, in the early evening, whether among the cooling trees in summer or when Lost Lagoon is edged in crisp sheets of winter ice, if you bend an ear and filter out the persistent mechanical hum of city life, you can sense the ghosts of those Stanley Park Zoo buffalo, seals, polar bears, calling out from their confining enclosures, rumbling in uneasy sleep.

Of all these spectres, the zoo's 1908 Monkey House (the one that concerns this book most) leaves the most palpable disturbance on the empty air. Replaced in the early 1950s by a modern structure which itself was razed at the zoo's closure, the Monkey House, at least physically, has disappeared as completely as last autumn's leaves. Yet the monkeys themselves, and one in particular, seem as if they will not quite fade away.

A wooden building that sat at one point of a triangle, the other two points made up of the gabled stone Stanley Park Pavilion and the children's playground, on the rise overlooking Pipeline Road, in style the Monkey House evoked those small-town railway depots where there are ticket windows and a porch with hard wooden benches. With its brooding hipped roof, the Monkey House truly looked like a place to buy your ticket and be off to someplace distant and interesting. Of course, it was no departure point for the primates within, other than when they died.

There were cages inside and cages outside, the latter affixed to "monkey doors"—wire-boxed apertures through which the monkeys could emerge from the building for some fresh air outside.

After the Stanley Park Rose Garden was laid out adjacent to the Monkey House in 1920, visitors could stroll among the roses, then climb the path to watch, close enough to touch, those monkeys who emerged from the building into these wire boxes.

You could enter the Monkey House as well, if not just to watch the dozen or so monkeys, then to see the macaws and cockatoos who were also caged there. Complaints would arise over the years from parents whose children were bitten by monkeys into whose cages it was far too easy to push an incautious finger, and from animal welfare groups concerned about the monkeys' care. And many would walk past the building holding kerchiefs to their noses to ward off the "high smell."

Had you taken a stroll to see the monkeys one summer's day in 1937, you would have found a cage in the Monkey House that curiously stood apart from the other enclosures. In it was a Javanese macaque. She had what was described as a "greeny-brown" pelt and penetrating golden eyes. "Trim, alert, dainty," it was said, of actions "smart and quick," the female stood a little under two feet tall.[4]

This alertness and daintiness set her apart from the other primates, and something else did too—her apparent familiarity with a discrete segment of human society. Most Sundays, the monkey was visited by middle-aged ladies, flouncing in the frills or squared off in the tailored jackets last fashionable in the late 1920s and early 1930s. These earnest behatted women belonged to art appreciation societies or were amateur artists themselves; most of them loved and were guardians of dogs, cats and birds. To the monkey they cooed or spoke kind words, proffering candy or boiled eggs through the bars of her cage. Recognizing them, the monkey would grow excited, then reach out a small black hand and eat the treats, afterward carefully cleaning her fingers and mouth. It may be that her eyes searched the women as if seeking someone who might be there, someone who never was.

The monkey had come a long way to end up here, an ocean apart from the Javanese jungle lagoon where she had been born some sixteen years earlier. She had experienced a great deal more life than most of the animals held in cages at Stanley Park Zoo, and more than most of the human public who came to stare and prod fingers at her and her fellow inmates as they fidgeted in their finite spaces. She had lived in a house, warmed herself at a fire, worn a colourful wardrobe. And she had had a name—Woo.

In that house near downtown Victoria, she had lived with an artist named Emily Carr. Fifty-one years old when she purchased the monkey in 1923, Carr had to that date still not found her stride or her voice as artist, or an audience for her art. This discovery, for such we may justly call it, did not occur until 1927, and her genius was not to be fully recognized till the years just prior to her death in 1945. The Sunday ladies who came with treats for Woo—friends, acolytes, believers in Carr's worth as an artist—were her proxies from Victoria, where the artist lay recovering from the series of heart attacks that had sent her monkey to this cage in the Monkey House of Stanley Park Zoo in the first place.

Woo had witnessed Carr's struggle as she trudged from obscurity to increasing renown. Indeed, it has always been my impression that this monkey served more than an incidental role in the process that freed the artist to sing with all her voice, paint with all her colours, to live free of fear—fear the artist held to be an absence of faith. For Carr, faith was more than a matter of religious devotion or positive thinking. It was one of the many gifts she recognized in the animals who were her closest companions. She had once mentioned as much to a friend. "The faith the animals have in us is heart-warming," she said, adding that it "exceeds by far the faith we have in each other."[5]

This monkey, and the other animals who were part of Carr's faithful household—the dogs, cats, birds and rodents—were the beings on whom the artist depended in a world of humans whom she believed did not comprehend or believe in her. Paradoxically, these animals would also, in future, consign that artist to the twilit carnival realm of a curious eccentric, sentimental subject for children's tales, a Pied Piper of Victoria, a human cartoon. As if love of animals made one naïve when, in fact, it made one very wise.

Irony always lies heavy in the air of zoos, and it was especially so with Woo. She had helped open the door to freedom for an artist whose work is in all respects a declaration of independence for the natural world, yet her own life was lived at the end of a chain and, at that life's end, boxed up for public display, returned not to the wild but to a stricter captivity, among other monkeys she did not know or recognize as her own species.

Her ordeal was not long. One Sunday, perhaps toward springtime 1938, Carr's friends came with their usual treats for the monkey, only to find her cage empty. "She died of old age," the zookeeper told them.[6]

He was wrong. Woo should have been in the prime of her life. The monkey lived to about seventeen, just over half of what her life expectancy would have been in the wild. A friend of the artist heard of a quite different, possibly more plausible cause of death. The monkey, she wrote, "had died, they said, of a broken heart."[7]

When I was a boy, growing up in a small California town in the late 1960s and early 1970s, I went through a phase of desperately wanting a pet monkey. In part, this was because I knew a lot about them. My parents ensured we had lots of picture books and encyclopedias to help us learn the ins and outs of the natural world. Along with these, we had something better than books: our home constituted a kind of private menagerie, with a pony, several dogs and cats, birds, hamsters, guinea pigs and mice, and an aquarium filled with the floating jewels of tropical fish.

What I really wanted, though, was a monkey. And it had to be a certain kind. It had to be a squirrel monkey. This was not so much due to my books as that I had fallen victim to a particularly cruel marketing tool. I had seen advertisements in boys' magazines that, in those bad old days, offered to send the buyer monkeys by post not from some South American jungle but from places in the southern United States, to wherever one lived, for an incredibly small amount of money. I remember one of them. Against a background of acid yellow, a squirrel monkey sat on an open human palm, dressed in a kind of suit. The "Darling Pet Monkey" could be yours for $18.95, with free collar, leash and cage. "Loads of fun and amusement," the ad promised. I confess that at that age, I thought only about how much fun it would be for me.[8]

I showed the ad to my mother and begged for the money to buy the "darling pet monkey." She advised me to forget about it. "Don't you know they ship them? How they die from the stress, from lack of air and water? No, honey. We won't do that to some poor creature."

I still didn't get it. I was about seven or eight, already keeping a diary. In it, I confessed my love for the monkey and offered prayer to some generalized interventionist divinity to give him to me. I fixed up part of my room for the "darling" monkey and got out my baby clothes, with which I would dress him. I would care for the monkey day and night; he would sleep with me and wake with me. What joy it would be—for me.

I didn't yet know, or consider, the tragedy that so often attends human interaction with primates, from the individual ones of monkeys made to perform in streets or sit in cages in zoos to the broader tragedy of primates, captured from the wild or bred for the purpose, for whom the fluorescent lighting and steel surfaces of labs, and daily subjection to stress and pain, is the only world, from start to finish, that they will ever know.

And then came a terrible awakening that changed my whole view of monkeys and, indeed, of all animals exploited for human uses. One day, when I was around nine years old, I was rummaging in some old *Life* magazines stacked in my father's workshop. When I found an issue featuring an article about a monkey, I grabbed it with excitement, sat down in the quiet dustiness to read, and a world of horror opened before me. The article contained pictures of a small monkey, perhaps a rhesus. The text in which these cute photographs swam was heart-stopping. In the clear-cut, clinical way of all laboratory test reports, the article described how the monkey was sedated, then how its head was removed and hooked up to tubes while being monitored for brain activity. I seem to recall reading that it actually opened its eyes. What was that bodiless, doomed consciousness like? We have some idea. According to those present, the head became distressed, angry, frantic. It lived only a few hours.

I have seen much worse images, read of equally horrible animal experiments, since then. But this glimpse of what I took to be the real world effectively shattered my childhood. I lay on the floor of Dad's workshop, sobbing, no longer a little boy and sobbing for that too. Waves of pity for the animal, anger at the scientists, existential agony, washed over me. I wanted to rescue monkeys from these torture chambers, end their unbearable state of incarceration and exploitation. And I, a child, could do nothing.

I was brought up to treat our animal family as just that—equal members of the nuclear household. They needed us, we needed them. It was symbiotic give and take. So when the news crashed upon my young heart that monkeys and other animals were put through laboratory tests for everything from dishwashing soap to life-saving cancer drugs, I could not un-know what I had learned. I held my dogs and cats closer to me, and all desire for a monkey was scoured out of my heart and mind. Monkeys, like performing elephants, belong where they came from—the wild—not under circus tents or on dissection tables or in somebody's house in British Columbia.

When I learned that Emily Carr had kept a monkey in her home, I oscillated between conflicting reactions. Part of me, reading Carr's own writings, saw the monkey as something of a victim, cast member of a sideshow the reclusive artist needed to surround herself with to distance herself from other humans, whom she could never trust, and never love, as she did her animal family, and also as an extra in the considerable drama of being Emily Carr, the sort of eccentric pet an eccentric artist would keep. And the other part of me was very much on Carr's side. I felt a oneness with her beyond the fact that we both loved our animal families. I understood her sense of alienation from the humans around her and her sense of oneness with the animals who loved her unconditionally. And I saw her need for family. After all, had I not also planned to dress my monkey in clothing, wake him and put him to bed, introduce him to my daily routines, a sort of child forever in my care? I could see Woo, in her colourful skirts, sewing a piece of cloth, controlled in everything she did, as a kind of daughter to Carr, a family member not foisted on her by fate in the ordinary way but a child she chose herself, perhaps for reasons as much to do with Carr's own need for freedom—for what animal is less amenable to restraint than a monkey?—as her desire for another animal to add to her private zoo.

And alongside this, I could see Woo as a kind of doppelgänger to Carr, one who could raise hell, and eyebrows, in free-flowing emotional displays, which Carr, child of the Victorian age and of peculiarly repressed parents, still made something of an effort to conceal. Woo's passions and predicaments were all about getting something she wanted, acting on impromptu urges, no matter the good people sitting in the parlour with their teacups, no matter the disapproval of Carr's sisters. Woo was a kind of creature whose very eccentricity drew people to her, even as Carr's own eccentricities pushed them away. "Emily Carr was not an introvert as many have claimed. Emily was an extrovert," Carr biographer and psychoanalyst Dr. Phyllis Marie Jensen told me. "Being an extrovert, she needed company, and preferably playful, creative company that would appreciate her and not judge her. She had been judged enough. And like all of us, she wanted to be loved."[9]

Carr was not unique in believing that the best love is that which comes to human beings from animals. She just went further than most and made it her life's credo.

Woo was, I surmised, an escape valve for Carr's passions, which even brush and paint, pen and paper, were inadequate to express. I also suspected something else. I had studied Carr's paintings and sketches of Indigenous art, specifically her depictions of totem poles, those deeply coded emblems of tribal history, legend and genealogy. Carr's early work in this regard is attractive, but as was pointed out by such keen critics as the American abstract expressionist painter Mark Tobey and Lawren Harris, one of the Canadian painters known collectively as the Group of Seven, they were mere copies of one art form transferred to another without much depth or interpretation. (Of course, Carr, who hoped to interest the BC government in her paintings as records of a vanishing world, had to contend with tin-eared bureaucrats who claimed her work was not photographic enough.) Later in Carr's career, Tobey and Harris each guided her toward an understanding of the principles of abstract art, as if to a land she'd never visited. But Carr had already visited this terra incognita on her journeys in northern British Columbia and Alaska. On Carr's visits to Indigenous communities, what she saw in the totems and long houses and masks and textiles was a different way of offering her vision of the natural world, through the lens of another culture. In these villages, she began to relinquish the strict rules of her formal art education, which was also the relinquishment of fears that had kept her subjugated to those rules. Abstract technique has its own laws, but what it offered Carr, when she was ready to embrace it, was a freedom she had not known. The Indigenous art of Vancouver Island, the northern British Columbia coast, Haida Gwaii and Alaska, with its free-form interpretations of animal and human figures and symbolic depictions of Indigenous ancestry and mythology, were to Carr what African masks were to Pablo Picasso. Though criticism has been levelled at her efforts as amounting to what we categorize today as cultural appropriation—and the challenge of just what the boundaries and ethics of cultural appropriation are continue to raise questions and controversy, around Carr's work and that of other artists similarly inspired—they made her see the world differently and thus depict it differently than she had done before, in ways that did not have to touch base with formal art-making principles.

Along with Tobey and Harris and totems and masks, I believe Woo had something to do with encouraging Carr's act of self-liberation, self-realization as artist and woman. One of Carr's greatest friends and mentors, Ira Dilworth, recognized Woo's significance to Carr the writer. When Carr was writing the stories collected in her book *The Heart of a Peacock,* Dilworth noted that in an early draft of her recollections of Woo, Carr seemed to get in the way of her own narrative. Carr, he wrote, was trying to make Woo interesting and, thus, cancelling herself out. "When you forget this," he went on, "and let Woo take charge of you and your style," the entire manuscript benefited and a certain magic unfolded in the narrative. Surely the same followed in her painting, too.[10]

As I know well, having animal family in one's life is as inspiring as it is healthy for heart and soul. But dogs, cats, even birds, don't bring to a domestic scene the impromptu energy of a monkey. Carr was never particularly comfortable depicting living forms—her portraits are technically superb and even arresting, if comparatively few in number. But along with the advice and attention of Tobey and Harris, the knee-high figure of Woo, gambolling about Carr's studio, stretching to reach or sitting with the tensile dignity of all primates, turning her golden eyes to gaze at her human "mother," her face a constantly shifting reflection of human emotions but sealed to human appeal, forever a mystery known only to the monkey—these factors, and perhaps just having at her beck and call a primate, that human figure in the abstract, had, I believe, a great deal to do with freeing Carr from the restraints that had held her in check as artist and as woman. For after Woo entered her life in 1923, doors and windows, formerly somewhat ajar in Carr's creative world, were not pushed out but blown open. We see an artist who has freed herself to be exactly who she wants, and needs, to be.

Monkeys had served as an archetype of fear for Carr, for reasons she does not explain but which I speculate were tied in with symbols of evil woven into the fabric of strict Calvinist religious faith. This faith had blanketed her all her childhood, added to which was the Victorian middle-class domestic decorum in which she was raised, every bit as strict as rules in church, which permitted no straying from the narrow way of devotion and duty. By definition, monkeys know no restraints: they scratch themselves, spit, freely giving vent to every urge, traits which may have been believed normal for the saloon-goers and sailors of whom the Carr family disapproved, but had absolutely no place in the parlours of "good society." This atmosphere of religion and propriety had worked a spell over Carr, one it took her years to awaken from as she realized her own potential and valued her own gifts even if the authority figures in her life did not. It seemed to me quite possible that Woo had helped break that spell and, in turn, helped Carr encourage others to broaden their own horizons and hearts. Her art, her writings, her life, continue to inspire us today with that same call to freedom.

As such, I wanted to know more about Woo. I wanted to see where she had lived, explore where she had died, know what others thought of her, figure out her relationship to a woman who adored her yet who, in a plot twist to their relationship that remains a dark mark on Carr's brilliant life, gave her away to a municipal zoo. I didn't want Woo to just disappear, along with the gently moaning spectres of captive buffalo or bears, with the Monkey House and its wild ghosts still watching and waiting among the neat rose beds of Stanley Park.

"As we live through these kaleidoscopic days when confusion, distrust, conflict and misery are so common everywhere," wrote journalist and animal rights pioneer J. Allen Boone, "it is revealing to note that more and more people are finding reassurance and peace of mind in companionship beyond the boundaries of humanity."[11] Written in 1954, Boone's words are even more applicable, and necessary, to our kaleidoscopic days of the early twenty-first century. Carr found in Woo that companionship across the boundaries of humanity, and through that companionship a fulfillment she needed—which we all need. Like the peacock Carr writes of, who bloomed in her friendly company yet faded and died in that of a public who paid to gaze on him behind the circumscribing bars of a zoo enclosure, Woo deserved, and deserves, better. All our animal family do.

PART I

The untold want, by life and land ne'er granted,
Now, Voyager, sail thou forth, to seek and find.

—Walt Whitman, *"The Untold Want"*

CHAPTER 1

"Scanted in a Dull Cage"

The leaded windows of the Empress hotel's wood-panelled library peered, as we did, at a perfect picture postcard view of the Inner Harbour, through panes slender as a slice of afternoon teacake. With nightfall, the panes reflected back to us the light of chandeliers inside the elegant room and a colourful party taking place there.

I had been invited to the party by Linda Rogers, poet laureate of Victoria and cousin of the Victorian poet Gerard Manley Hopkins, he who wrote of the spirit of man in terms of an animal seeking freedom, "As a dare-gale skylark scanted in a dull cage."[12] We were among some three dozen people gathered to celebrate the funding, creation and eventual raising of a statue dedicated to artist Emily Carr, who for too long had been scanted in her own dull cage when it came to a public memorial in the city of her birth.

A maquette—a small-scale model of the bronze statue-to-be of Carr—stood on a heavy oak table in the library, presided over by actress Molly Raher Newman impersonating the artist. Carr's hairnet, the grey and black workaday clothing that made Gertrude Stein look a fashion plate, and her sardonic smile, all recreated by Newman, are echoed in the maquette, itself inspired by a famous photograph of Carr. Carr's friend, painter Nan Cheney, took the photo of Carr in her Simcoe Street garden in 1930, her pet monkey, Woo, on her right shoulder, one of her Brussels griffon dogs cradled in her left arm. Carr smiles but Woo, wearing collar and chain but not her signature frock, sits brooding, eating something, perhaps uncomfortable as the centre of attention, unhappy sharing Carr with Cheney, or both. The sculptor, Barbara Paterson of Edmonton, creator of the Famous

Five statue in Ottawa, took artistic licence to its natural conclusion, omitting the griffon and placing at Carr's feet her bobtail sheepdog, Billie, raising his head for a scruff; adding the frock to Woo; and seating Carr on a rock, the most elemental furniture possible for this celebrant of the wild poetry of British Columbia's natural world. The completed statue now stands on the corner of Government and Belleville Streets on Empress hotel property, facing the Inner Harbour, where it is rarely to be seen without a small crowd of Carr fans and selfie-seekers surrounding it, Billie's head rubbed shiny with passing affection.

The story of how this striking, and overdue, statue finally came to be is a lengthy one. No one would be blamed for wondering why the province of British Columbia, or indeed the nation of Canada, had not already erected such a statue in Victoria years before. The reason that is so is that Carr is still viewed by many in and outside of Victoria as a sort of dotty old auntie who pushed her pets around in a pram and just happened to paint some immortal pictures along the way. Part of this impression is understandable, because I well know that even those who see Carr as a dotty old auntie also revere her as one of Canada's greatest artists, and in that strange antechamber between truth and fiction anyone may come to grips with a genius even if she does carry a monkey on her shoulder to do the week's shopping. It should be said, though, that Carr was much more than a character—some might say she was much more than an artist. "A force of nature" fits her pretty well, and is a title of which I like to think she would have been proud.

The Emily Carr Statue Fund was born in 2004 through the efforts of the Parks and Recreation Foundation of Victoria. Two years later, the province ponied up five thousand dollars. The model of the statue was unveiled in 2007, and a year later, British Columbia found another fifteen thousand to donate to the statue project. Saanich–Gulf Islands MP Gary Lunn lobbied the federal government for a large slice of the needed funds, and more support came from Calgary, then awash in oil cash, and sources back east. Actress Clarice Evans, a friend of the sculptor who was active in Hollywood's Golden Age and once the roommate of Marilyn Monroe, contributed twenty thousand dollars, the only woman to make such a gift.[13] This brings us back to August 2008, as I stood in the Empress library with Linda Rogers and fellow guests, raising our champagne glasses to the hard-won success of the endeavour, to celebrate that there was to be a memorial to Emily at last.

Victoria does not lack for other bronzed immortals. The city has its namesake luminary, Queen Victoria, who squints imperially over the Inner Harbour from the top of a granite plinth. For other figures, you have to dig into Google to find out what brought them to this metallic state of public veneration: Captain James Cook, the first European explorer to set foot on Vancouver Island, is one example of these. But for many decades there was no monument in Victoria to Carr, aside from a small stone footbridge—a fond but characteristically practical memorial—erected by her sister Alice Carr in 1945, the year of Emily's death, in Beacon Hill Park.

Victoria is justly famed for its references to vestiges of the lost British Empire, in the form of tea shops, flower baskets, that statue of Queen Victoria and money-making anachronisms like horse-drawn carriage rides. These are, after all, powerful tools of the tourist trade. But it is just as true that when people around the world think of Victoria, they also think of something else. They think of Emily Carr's stunning artworks, each stroke and colour suffused with living breath, even if they don't recognize her as the artist: *Indian Church* (1929), or *Big Raven* (1931), or *A Rushing Sea of Undergrowth* (1932–35). Those who read think of her literary works, in which she wielded a pen with as much genius as she did her paintbrush. There are those, myself among them, who would consider these more than enough of a monument to a creative artist. Still, the absence of something palpable, something people could visit without trudging to an art gallery, pose with, be inspired by, remained, and troubled some people in Victoria and elsewhere. It was a situation that might have amused Carr, all too familiar with being a prophet without honour in her own town.

Who was this artist with a monkey on her shoulder? Born on December 13, 1871 in the James Bay neighbourhood of Victoria, on a street named for her family (later changed to Government Street), Emily Carr was the fifth daughter of Richard Carr, an Englishman who had made a small fortune selling staples to gold miners in California before building a tall, Italianate house in a suburb of what would become British Columbia's capital city and settling his large family into its spacious rooms. Emily was the eighth of nine children, and the first of the family to be born after Confederation. She was thus a true Canadian, but also a true daughter of colonial privilege. At the farthest outskirts of the British Empire, where the pink map stopped at the edge of the Pacific Ocean, she had drawing and music lessons and was her father's pet, accompanying him everywhere until, still in childhood, she began to ask herself why she was treating him like a god—a question she was to ask herself about many a fellow human being, but one she never asked of Nature: she (Carr's preferred third-person pronoun when referring to Earth) remained sacred to her, not to be pestered with questions but celebrated as the visible source of ultimate goodness more conventionally religious folks ascribed to a hoped-for heaven.

Carr seemed to have been born to be disappointed in life as it presented itself, her world from childhood till old age punctuated by sudden moments of elated revelation followed by abject doubt. It was indeed a tragedy that she lost her mother in her sensitive teens. Emily saw fragile Mrs. Carr as a kind of visiting angel, not meant to spend much time among earthly beings. Emily Saunders Carr was clearly a loving woman with a free imagination. One of daughter Emily's most enchanting and moving pieces of writing is her description of sharing a picnic with her mother, who though ill with the tubercular cough that presaged her death, was heard to tell the family's minister that if her voice had given out, at least her heart sang. According to Emily, Mrs. Carr's heart also sang for her, with breath she could scarcely spare, those few hours among the white lilies of Richard Carr's field. It was Carr's last private time with her mother, who died of consumption shortly afterward, in 1886. From that point on, it seems to me, Carr was on the hunt not for another mother but for something to love and mother herself. Animals, those childlike beings so easy to put under human control and cast in roles pleasing to their human, about which they had no choice, became her focus. They were, indeed, reflections of herself. And it is clear she yearned to treat them and love them as she herself would have liked to have been treated and loved, trusting them as she would have liked to have been able to trust humans.

Richard Carr also died of consumption, in November 1888, after mourning Mrs. Carr for two years. He may have also been grieving the death of his formerly close relationship with his daughter Emily. Sometime in 1883, when Emily was eleven or twelve years old, Richard Carr had made what is thought to have been an attempt to explain the facts of life to his daughter. Something about the conversation mysteriously left Emily devastated then and for the rest of her life. It was an event that she afterward referred to cryptically as the "brutal telling" and blamed for the estrangement that fell between her and her father. (This event remains enigmatic to Carr scholars.) Yet she forever celebrated his one great gift to her: his love of birds and of all animals. It would be easy to ascribe this to sentimentality, but if we do so we do her and her animal family a disservice, for animals were the fulcrum of Carr's greatness. They were what allowed Emily Carr to become, magnificently, the artist and writer she was meant to be, the woman who inspires us today. It was the one bit of purity Emily was still willing to accord Richard Carr after the "brutal telling." Animals remained the reliable, neutral bridge that crossed even the deepest canyons between one person and another.

Carr's career as an artist moved along slowly, at a pace chosen as if by traversing a room in darkness. If she trusted animals, she did not trust people, nor even herself or her talent, at least in the beginning and for far too long. She studied art in California, in England and in France, and was older than many of the students beside her. With a keen eye for the art techniques she admired, Carr was able to pick up French impressionism with admirable results, but her own individual voice was not to be heard in any of these early canvases. She travelled north of Vancouver Island, spending time in the Indigenous communities along the mainland coast, sketching people and totems in what she saw as a race against time, because both the people of the region and their cultural artefacts were fading away.

Yet it was never clear, especially to Carr, whether she was appropriating Indigenous art forms as her own, in the naïve, well-meant but ultimately unoriginal style of an anthropologist collecting data, or presenting to the world a unique body of work. She was, at the same time, paddling a figurative canoe into dark and uncharted waters, seeking her own artistic way.

In the meantime, Carr had to make a living. In 1913, she built and ran an apartment building she called Hill House and which, in her 1944 memoir about her life as landlady, she dubbed "The House of All Sorts." Originally conceived to offer two rentable suites, with living space and studio for Carr, the interior of Hill House had to be subdivided over time to create additional units, as Carr found her venture not as lucrative as she had dreamed. Increasing rentable space meant adding to the number of potential tenants, perhaps as many as a dozen at a time when business was good. But with good business came the stress of dealing with the needs of people, and in the financial slump after World War I, even increasing the number of tenants did not add much to Carr's income. So another of her money-making efforts was the breeding of English bobtail sheepdogs and, later, Brussels griffons. Without doubt, this sideline was far more agreeable to Carr than the hectic sideshow of being a landlady. As she confided to her journal in 1934, "Heaven forgive me.

How I hate tenants."[14] Heaven forgave her. Animals, nature, a broad notion of a godhead embracing a universe of infinite goodness, and many pains dealt her heart here on Earth, none of them fatal but none forgettable, and some unforgiveable—these were what kept Emily Carr going through the worst life could throw at her, rather like another Emily she brings to mind, which I was keen to share with Linda Rogers as we studied Barbara Paterson's maquette on the table before us in the Empress library.

"I've always seen Emily Carr as our Emily Dickinson," I said to her.

"Yes," she said, nodding. "Loved animals and flowers. Could do without people, except for those few monolithic, mythic beings she revered beyond reason or reality. Was considered nutty in Amherst, as Carr was in Victoria. Was most honoured after her death. Yes, I see it."

"And while her genius has been recognized around the world," I continued, "she is still regarded by some as just that, Squire Dickinson's half-cracked daughter. She didn't mingle, she loved birds and flowers, she kept her own society, and so must be half-cracked. And, what's worse, *cute*. The way Walt Whitman is never seen as cute, or Tom Thomson."

"Ugh," Linda agreed, taking a sip of champagne. "Poetry is a strange thing. You either get it or you don't. Those that get it can't always tell those that don't why they get it, because the art form reaches places inside them where, paradoxically, words can't convey the ecstasy they cause. And, too, a lot of those who don't get it think poets and poetasters are nuts to begin with. Our Emily was double trouble: a painter *and* a poet."

"Was Carr nuts?" I asked.

Oh no, she assured me, with emphasis. "Wasn't it Dickinson who said, 'Much madness is divinest sense?' Carr had a very different, very special way of seeing her world. She was a vessel not without its flaws. But what she spilled over for our eyes to enjoy—that is divinest sense, I think."

But the animals, I persisted. Did Linda see my point? That Carr's menagerie, a potent source of inspiration, was ironically one of the factors that lowered her standing when she and her oeuvre were compared with the Group of Seven (that all-male fellowship of Canadian landscape painters) in the eyes of self-styled art aficionados inclined to see her as a "lady artist" with the numerous dogs and cats of the bona fide eccentric. It was a sexist thing too, I went on. Few male artists, to my knowledge, are given the same treatment because of the pets they love. When was the last time you read a "crazy cat lady" (or dog lady) send up of Charles Dickens, or Pablo Picasso, or Richard Wagner? It seemed to me only women were judged negatively by the kinds and numbers of pets they included in their private lives. How was that fair?

"I remember reading that Carr, for some reason, was afraid of monkeys," Linda said. "Perhaps Woo gave her permission to exorcise whatever monkey demons haunted her?"

As we listened to the pleasant conversations around us, the tinkling of wine glasses and the murmurs of waitstaff offering hors d'oeuvres, Linda's words rang through my mind, and I recalled a conversation from many years before. An acting teacher friend of mine had told me what he said to his students on their first day of class. "Get inside and confront the things you fear," he told them. "If it's your mom, or dad, or the goldfish that died when you were five, deal with it. Something you did that you can't forgive yourself for, face it. If you're gay and hiding it—don't creep out of that closet. Leap out. Because you will never reach the heights or the depths if you are not honest with your audience and, especially, with yourself. And believe me when I say you will never be the artist you could have been."

Linda thought that a reasonable corollary. "Remember Chekhov's advice to actors?" she asked me. "'If you want to work on your art, work on your life.'" She added, "There have been many artists, writers and so on, over history, whose lives were enriched by animals they loved. Why shouldn't Woo have served that role for Carr?"

I knew there were many such artists, fine, serious, important artists. Frida Kahlo. Pablo Picasso. Jackson Pollock. Georgia O'Keeffe. Dogs, cats, birds, monkeys had been there in the studio as the artist painted or pondered, with a regularity and fidelity that may not have been acknowledged, but whose presence, any of these artists might point out, made all the difference. I knew the inspirational power of an animal from my own dog, Freddie. How many late nights and early mornings had he sat by me as I wrestled with materials for a book project, his soft brown eyes looking up at mine when, head in hands, I straightened up to begin the struggle all over again. Novelist Edith Wharton, whose fiction is full of greater and nobler truths about the condition of women in a man's world and the cruelties of the social order than many who read it realize, called her dog "a heartbeat at my feet."

Was Woo that heartbeat to Emily Carr? And what was Emily Carr to Woo?

"If I were you," Linda told me, smiling like a canny Raphael cherub, "I would get busy finding out."

CHAPTER 2

The Gamekeeper's Daughter

Likely born between 1921 and 1923 in the wild somewhere on the island of Java in Indonesia, the monkey who became Woo belonged to a widely dispersed primate group called crab-eating macaques (*Macaca fascicularis*).[15] Macaques do not live entirely on crustaceans, though; these omnivores will eat just about anything, including small birds, eggs, fish and whatever they can coerce or steal. This eclectic diet is ideal for monkeys who have chosen to live near humans for millennia, in roles ranging from temple guardians to agricultural pests, in settings rural and urban. But as these monkeys might well tell us if they could, the choice to stick close to humans has been a double-edged sword.

Woo and her mother—for young macaques and their mothers are never separate by choice—most likely started out not far from the lowland coast of western Java, close enough to the shoreline to forage for fish or crustaceans and near enough to trees and vines to escape predators. Their natural habitat was also increasingly encroached upon by humankind. Colonized by the Dutch since the early seventeenth century, Indonesia had become a major producer of everything from rubber to pepper to tobacco and sugar. Indeed, by the 1920s, Java ranked with Cuba for sugar production and the industry expanded throughout the decade. The Dutch East India Company eventually turned Java into one huge plantation under colonial rule, with the native population subjugated, often brutally, to service Dutch debts and stockholder expectations. Wildlife also paid the price for colonial resource exploitation as plantations devoured available land.

The exotic animal trade was then, as now, a way for the local population of disenfranchised poor to survive in foreign-controlled areas with depressed local economies. It is possible that Woo was captured by someone living in the area near where she lived, specifically for sale abroad.

Woo was shipped to North America in 1922 or 1923, and this brings us to a double-windowed store front of plain painted brick on Government Street in Victoria containing a pet store run by a Scottish-Canadian woman, the shop's windows filled with caged puppies, birds and monkeys.

How many of us, as we bring home a dog or cat adopted from a shelter, don't wonder about our pet's prior history? Journalist Kim Kavin, in *Little Boy Blue: A Puppy's Rescue from Death Row and His Owner's Journey for Truth*, went further than wondering: she traced her rescue pup's trajectory back to the unscrupulous breeder he'd been born to and then to one of the most death-dealing kill shelters on the eastern American seaboard, extrapolating from Blue's past that of all the unwanted dogs like him, most were not as lucky as he was to be rescued. Kavin's was no easy journey, meeting the larger tragedy of an outdated, heartless system and the individual tragedies of dogs who had not managed to survive it.

It is a challenging exercise in creative nonfiction, bordering on pure fiction, to try to get inside the mind of an animal and learn about what it has endured. An animal's experience can be pondered, guessed at, put to the methodical determinations of science. We will never know; they will never tell us. But we can guess, as Virginia Woolf did when she wrote her life of Flush, the spaniel companion of Elizabeth Barrett Browning, from his days spent in the ill poet's London bedroom to his death in old age at her feet in an Italian city. "But what is 'oneself?'" Woolf had Flush wonder as he gazed at himself in Miss Barrett's looking-glass. "Is it the thing people see? Or is it the thing one is?"[16]

We know the young female macaque arrived in Victoria with several other monkeys; whether they all belonged to the same species is not clear though implied in Carr's account, and we also know that she had made another stop before her Canadian arrival. In a 1923 article in the *Daily Colonist*, Victoria's paper of record, it was pointed out that the pet store where Carr was to find Woo, located at 1316 Government Street (the Russell Building), received its monkeys only after they had spent a lengthy period in the United States. "They come from Java, by way of San Francisco, in which port they are acclimatized for three months before coming north."[17] What this acclimatization entailed I do not know. It may refer to quarantine.

According to the article, Mrs. A.G. Cowie, née Lucy Henderson Alexander, wife of Alfred G. Cowie, opened the Bird and Pet Shop in 1921 (which was incidentally also the year in which the United States quarantine system was nationalized—prior to which quarantine stations were locally administered).[18] This does not seem to have harmed Mrs. Cowie's trade. "All the tourists seem to find the shop," she told a reporter, "and that is good for business." It was noted that the pedigreed dogs she offered were especially interesting to Americans as there was no duty charged on them.[19]

Daughter of the gamekeeper on an estate in Perthshire, Scotland, and formerly in domestic service herself, Lucy Cowie had grown up surrounded by animals, albeit animals as pastime and commodity.[20] Arriving in Canada in 1920 with her Canadian-born husband, she had opened her pet shop in Victoria soon after, and seems to have run it successfully until she and Alfred moved to Vancouver in the mid-1930s.[21]

Lucy's attitude regarding the sale of wild animals might have evolved over the years, given her later friendship with Lilian Marion Rigby Russell, London-born daughter of an anti-slavery British consul at Zanzibar and herself a leading socialist of her day who owned fruit orchards in the Kootenays. An associate of Dr. Albert Schweitzer, with whom she worked in Africa and whose sermons and books she translated into English, Russell had rescued and returned to the wild many injured or abandoned monkeys. In her 1938 book, *My Monkey Friends*, Russell stated unequivocally, "I trust this little book has not made anybody wish to go out and buy a monkey, for by doing so they would encourage a horrible form of trade—the trade in wild animals." Presumably by 1948, with *My Monkey Friends* in her hands, Lucy Cowie realized her selling of monkeys in Victoria had been horrible too.[22]

In the mid-1920s, however, not so much. The Bird and Pet Shop's innocuous shingle concealed a fairly diverse trade in exotic animals. Alongside the puppies and kittens displayed in its front windows were parrots from Panama, Chinese mockingbirds and Australian cockatoos—and of course, primates. No wonder, as Carr tells us, Mrs. Cowie endured headaches because of all the customs paperwork. The prices on the monkeys, according to what Mrs. Cowie told the *Colonist*, ranged from $25 to $30—which, in today's loonies, is somewhere between $350 and $400. So whatever the headaches brought on by customs men and the nationalization of US quarantine, Mrs. Cowie must have found herself doing very well indeed.[23]

Arriving at 1316 Government Street in a crate with the other monkeys, into which they had been nailed in San Francisco after a ninety-day spell spent somewhere in that city and, before that, surviving a sail across the Pacific in the belly of a ship, Woo would probably have been frightened to be let out of what may have seemed the only safe place she knew.

Shipments of exotic animals to feed a burgeoning and lucrative trade had always been fraught with misery and danger for the living commodity stored in the hold. In the late nineteenth century, not so long before Carr had travelled to London in 1899 to study art, animals purchased from "collectors" who had captured them in Africa and Asia sometimes never reached the docks in England, thanks to disease contracted in crowded conditions, injuries from being tossed in storms, or even from going down with capsized ships, like the four elephants and three tigers British wildlife dealer Charles Jamrach had purchased for sale in 1873.[24]

Even Danish writer Karen Blixen (writing under the *nom de plume* Isak Dinesen), who in her day had shot at least one of every exotic animal she could find on her African safaris, recognized the particular horror of fragile wild creatures commodified, packed up and shipped like plunder from the only home they had known, beginning a journey they might not survive. She once caught a glimpse of two giraffes, heads poking up from their crates, being prepared for shipment from Mombasa to the Hamburg Zoo in Germany. "They could not know or imagine the degradation toward which they were sailing," Blixen wrote. She prayed they would die before they reached their cold, callous, commercial destination.[25]

Since Woo was only one or two years old when she arrived at Lucy Cowie's pet shop (apparently the youngest of the captives there), she must have endured not only capture and confinement but separation far too early from her mother. As Viktor Reinhardt of the Animal Welfare Institute wrote, "Once the mother stops nursing the infant for good, the affectionate bond between the two is not broken. The young usually remain in the maternal group at least until the age of puberty."[26] If Woo really was two years old when Carr met her, she had been weaned for only a year. As studies have proved, young monkeys separated from their mothers too soon are set up for a number of unique syndromes, including increased aggression, a reduced ability to fight off infections and a lifespan shorter than would be expected in the wild.[27]

In *The Heart of a Peacock*, Carr wrote that Mrs. Cowie, a busy and canny businesswoman, was at wits' end because the special cage she was having built for the shipment of monkeys was not yet ready for them. As the dazed, excited monkeys dashed around the shop, having not always friendly encounters with the other animals caged there, Mrs. Cowie hit on a solution. Putting an old adage to good practical use, she found and rolled in an empty barrel, removed its top and hammered an unused parrot cage over the opening. Then, one by one, she fed into the barrel each of the monkeys, finally fastening the cage door shut against their grasping black hands.[28]

In her published recollections of Woo, Carr didn't elaborate on how she came to visit the shop of Mrs. Cowie, other than to state that she knew her well. This leaves the reader to envision her strolling past the shop one day and walking in on the spur of the moment, though this doesn't square with what we know of Carr's nature, which was not to act on the spur of the moment in anything. The 1923 *Colonist* article stated that only one monkey was left from Mrs. Cowie's recent shipment, and Carr writes of first seeing Woo among a whole barrel of them. This suggests that Carr had heard, perhaps at Mrs. Cowie's prompting, that a new shipment was just in, and came downtown expressly to look. But why did Carr come to have a look at them? After all, from her earliest childhood she had equated monkeys with devils and darkness. In one of her posthumously published anecdotes of her youth in Victoria, Carr related how, at the age of five or six, she and her siblings were roused from sleep by a ruckus on the porch of their father's house. It was the children of a neighbour on Menzies Street, Richard Wolfenden, who had come running for help. They had been bitten by a monkey that had broken loose in the neighbourhood and "terrorized" them while their parents were out. (Richard and Emily Carr were also out that evening.)[29] The monkey belonged to a woman, Mrs. William Lush, who owned The Colonist Hotel, then located at 200 Douglas Street, just across from one of Richard Carr's fields in James Bay.[30]

Carr had already met, if just from a distance, this monkey and others kept by Mrs. Lush. She did not keep the monkeys chained, and as a result they often invaded Richard Carr's fields, where Emily watched them with trembling fascination. To her, with a vivid imagination that blurred the boundary between reality and fantasy, it was as if they were demonic beings. "I got them associated with the devil," Carr wrote. "I gave to them supernatural powers" to such a degree she became obsessed with keeping her feet from touching the lower part of her bed at night, because she feared that their human-like hands, which "could open doors," might be down there in the dark.[31] Carr may have been influenced by attitudes toward primates current in her parents' highly religious home. Though they were often to be found in the arms of royal princesses and chained to the thrones of kings, since ancient times monkeys were seen by the Christian church as a *Simia Dei* or the "Monkey of God," a sort of parody of Satan.[32] Later on, monkeys were feared for their reputed unbridled lust, another characteristic with which the average devout Christian wanted nothing to do. (Although there were, as in all religious matters, exceptions: Canadian medieval historian Margaret Wade Labarge noted in her authoritative study of life in a thirteenth-century baronial household that many of the important medieval clerics of Europe kept a monkey as a way of distracting themselves from the weight of their spiritual duties and political cares—perhaps, too, as a symbol of having finally put the devil in shackles.)[33]

One couldn't blame decent, morally upright people like Richard Carr for conflating the evil of the monkey with the purported evils of the Lush family's saloon. For that family had committed one of the worst of Victorian sins when they purchased the lot from Richard Carr in 1863—they had lied. Richard Carr had asked the Lushes to promise never to build a public house on the property they bought from him. William Lush agreed to the deal, recalled Emily Carr, only to renege and set up a saloon considered one of the most disreputable in town.[34] (A darker facet of Lush's persona was revealed when he fatally swallowed poison in January 1875, depressed that he was unable to pay a fine.)[35]

The Colonist Hotel likely was no noisier than any other such establishment, but because it served liquor, and the family could clearly hear sailors singing on their way to its door, fresh from the naval base at Esquimalt, the establishment devilishly haunted Richard Carr's nights—and, by extension, those of his family—till the day he died.[36] The monkeys became part of that nightmarish combination of inebriation (with all the attendant vices) and unseemly joie de vivre that made these unfettered half-beast, half-humans appear as if they were Mrs. Lush's minions, breaking free of the confines

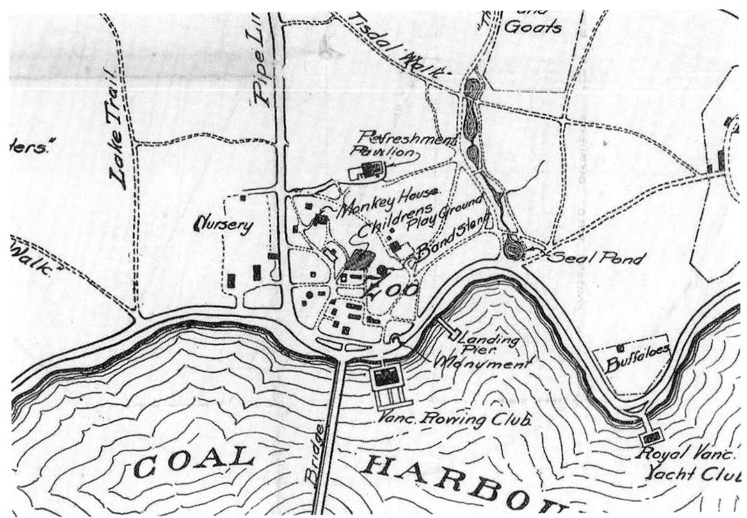

This detail from a 1911 map of Stanley Park shows the location of the Monkey House in the zoo. Stanley Park Zoo started out small, with a few bears, raccoons and donated pet monkeys in the 1880s, moving on to include polar bears, penguins and flamingos before it was shut down by popular demand—and an increasing number of scandals around animal welfare—in the 1990s. *City of Vancouver Archives,* MAP368B-r

The 1908 Stanley Park Monkey House, designed by fashionable Vancouver architect W.H. Archer, is featured in this vintage postcard. Located roughly between the Stanley Park Pavilion and the children's playground, this iteration of the Stanley Park Zoo's Monkey House was razed in the 1950s. *Image courtesy of Jolene Cumming*

A teenaged Emily with a crow friend on her arm at a family picnic. Sister Alice and brother Richard are seated at right. The woman at far left may be sister Lizzie.
Image I-60890 courtesy of the Royal BC Museum and Archives

This photo of Emily and her sisters seems to show how poorly her wild nature suited her conventional family. Clockwise from bottom centre: Alice, Lizzie, Edith, Clara and Emily.
Image A-02037 courtesy of the Royal BC Museum and Archives

This photograph shows Victoria Harbour, as viewed from the Parliament buildings designed by Francis Rattenbury, between 1902 and 1911. *Photo courtesy of Grant Hayter-Menzies*

Emily Carr in 1918 in the private back garden of her apartment house on Simcoe Street in Victoria, surrounded by her beloved animal family. *Image C-05229 courtesy of the Royal BC Museum and Archives*

Emily Carr and Woo pose together in the private garden behind her apartment house.
Carr's dress suggests she and Woo are hosting a garden party.
Image G-02845 courtesy of the Royal BC Museum and Archives

The Russell Building at 1316–1328 Government Street in Victoria was the site of Lucy Cowie's Bird and Pet Shop, which was located in the space that now has an awning reading "Seed of Life." *Photo courtesy of Joe Mabel*

This portrait taken circa 1935 shows Emily Carr with two griffons, her cat, Dolf, and Woo. According to Carr, Woo saved Dolf's life by alerting her to the injured cat, who was lying under a shrub after being hit by a car. Thanks to Woo, Dolf lived for many more years. *Unknown, [Photograph of Emily Carr], 1935–1945. Gelatin silver print, 8.8 × 10.7 cm. Art Gallery of Ontario, LA.SC024.114. © 2018 Art Gallery of Ontario*

Stopping by Lucy Cowie's pet shop in 1923, Carr described what she first saw of Woo: "a pathetic little face" with "surprised Kewpie hair" that stood up between two elfin ears. This photograph of Carr and Woo was taken in Victoria a few years after the monkey came to live with the artist at her boarding house in Victoria. *Image I-61505 courtesy of the Royal BC Museum and Archives*

This view of Vancouver and its harbour was photographed between 1902 and 1911, when Emily Carr taught and worked in her studio on Granville Street. *Photo courtesy of Grant Hayter-Menzies*

Emily had the Elephant, her beloved caravan, towed to scenic spots so she could paint and commune with nature and her animal family. Woo can be seen on her knee. *Image D-03844 courtesy of the Royal BC Museum and Archives*

St. Joseph's Hospital in Victoria, as seen from the gardens of St. Ann's Academy. Emily Carr was brought here in January 1937 after a series of heart attacks made it impossible for her to recover at home. Her illness also broke up her animal family. It was from St. Joseph's that she wrote the letter to the Stanley Park Zoo asking that the Monkey House take Woo. *Grant Hayter-Menzies photo*

Carr painted this portrait of Woo in about 1930. The monkey wears a stylized version of the smock Emily dressed her in for outdoor excursions in windy James Bay.
Image PDP00603 courtesy of the Royal BC Museum and Archives

Emily Carr's final portrait of Woo is untitled, perhaps unfinished (as may be indicated by the change of position of the tail), and also one of the last paintings from Carr's brush. She was working on it not long before her death in March 1945, seven years after Woo died in Stanley Park Zoo. *Emily Carr portrait of Woo, c. 1932 oil on wove paper, mounted on plywood, 90.5 × 59 cm Gift of Peter Bronfman, 1990 National Gallery of Canada, Ottawa Photo:* NGC

Story Book Farm Primate Sanctuary in Sunderland, Ontario, provides a home for rescued primates, many of whom are recovering from pain and neglect at the hands of humans. This view from the driveway shows the farmhouse and, at left, the barn annex where the primate residents live. *Grant Hayter-Menzies photo*

Gerdie (above) and Boo are captured investigating a light snow while their enclosure is cleaned. Retired from lives spent being experimented on in biomedical research, the pair are now residents at Story Book Farm. *Grant Hayter-Menzies photo*

Born in April 1992, Pockets Warhol is the famed monkey artist of Story Book Farm. A former pet in British Columbia, Pockets arrived at the sanctuary in fall 2009 and began painting shortly afterward. First exhibited in Toronto in 2011, Pockets's work is widely collected around the world, and sales of his paintings are a significant fundraiser for the sanctuary. *Photo courtesy of Charmaine Quinn*

Woo by Pockets Warhol, 2017. This painting, created by capuchin artist Pockets Warhol and named for Emily Carr's monkey muse, was presented to me at Story Book Farm Primate Sanctuary. I see many things in it—a golden butterfly, splashes of red that could be passion or pain. What I treasure most is the artist's rare handprint (seen to the right). *Photo courtesy of Grant Hayter-Menzies*

In the gallery at Story Book Farm, artist Anita Kunz (left), Pockets Warhol's muse Charmaine Quinn (right) and I are surrounded by Pockets's artwork as well as art donated for auction by prominent Canadian and American artists to benefit the sanctuary.
Photo courtesy of Daina Liepa

The memorial stone at Emily Carr's grave in Ross Bay Cemetery, Victoria, displays a quotation from *Hundreds and Thousands*. Note the small plaque with an illustration of a monkey, one of several mementos left by Carr admirers. *Grant Hayter-Menzies photo*

The author's copy of Lilian M. Russell's *My Monkey Friends*, inscribed at Christmas 1948 to Lucy Cowie, owner of Victoria's Bird and Pet Shop on Government Street. Lucy Cowie sold Woo to Emily Carr in 1923. *Grant Hayter-Menzies photo*

Emily Carr spent many years as a vexed landlady in her apartment house on Simcoe Street in Victoria. The second-storey windows of her studio are visible at the top right of photo, and the three small windows at basement level to the left are where Woo spent sunny days in winter, on view to all who passed in the street. *Grant Hayter-Menzies photo*

The private garden behind Carr's apartment house still contains Woo's gnarled and elderly apple tree, which can be seen just behind the ferns. The "basket" cedar is also a survivor from Carr's lifetime. *Grant Hayter-Menzies photo*

This passageway was used by Carr and Woo to travel between the two attics at Hill House. There are still marks in the board at the rear of the photo, which were made by Woo's nails as she swung herself over to join Carr. *Grant Hayter-Menzies photo*

Carr used this wall in her attic to catalogue her griffon dogs' ages and weight over time, starting in 1923, the year Woo came into her life. *Grant Hayter-Menzies photo*

One of Carr's painted eagles still remains on the underside of the attic roof at Hill House. She told her young friend Carol Pearson that these birds would protect her while she slept. *Grant Hayter-Menzies photo*

Barbara Paterson's memorial statue of Emily Carr—complete with dog Billie at her feet and Woo on her shoulder—stands at the corner of Belleville and Government Streets in Victoria's Inner Harbour, flanked by the British Columbia Parliament buildings and the Fairmont Empress hotel. Billie's head and Woo's exposed arm and tail are rubbed bright from the constant touch of passersby. *Photo courtesy of Les Hayter*

of her hellish establishment to wreak havoc throughout the rest of Richard Carr's placid little piece of pretend England.

Emily Carr had had in childhood a first-hand experience that led her to view saloons as places that subverted the strict social and racial hierarchies of colonial Victoria and the established rules of decency as set forth by Richard Carr. She claimed in later life, in an account that sounds like a soul's journey to and from the underworld, that as a child she had actually been inside one of Victoria's raucous taprooms, those places her father so abhorred. Wandering downtown, she had gotten caught up in a cattle stampede, as common an occurrence in Carr's childhood as traffic jams are there now. Just before the beasts could run Carr down, she remembered, she was carried to the safety of a nearby saloon. She found that her rescuer was a black man. Keenly aware of otherness and the price exacted for being different—Chinese servants who worked for white families and were repaid with indifference, Indigenous peoples whose land and dignity had been stolen—Carr remembered the man's broad smile and muscular arms as he sat her on a barstool and swallowed a whiskey while they waited until the cattle passed. The stranger then gently sent the little girl out on the wooden sidewalk in the settling dust, back to her own "respectable" world of James Bay.[37]

Otherness was both virtue and vexation for Carr, one she understood to a degree compatible with her own experiences of being outside the mainstream, and one that troubled her. Even as it set her gloriously apart from her conventional sisters, as one example, it also set her apart from everyone else, making her an outlier. This equivocal status made her quick to sympathize with others who did not fit in. "A lunatic, a prostitute, and a Chinese artist—these are among my friends," she wrote with satisfaction in her journal in August 1934. And this sympathy extended to animals forced to serve human uses.[38] This compassion for and camaraderie with society's perceived oddballs seems as if it should have included monkeys early on, but that revelation was to come later, because Carr's fear of primates was to take years to conquer.

Only as an adult, Carr wrote, during her art student days in London, did she let herself be taken by a friend to the area where the monkeys were kept at London Zoo in Regent's Park, and learn not to flee but "give the monkeys stare for stare and let them stroke my hand." She also forced herself to go into London pet shops to study the monkeys there—indeed, one of the most prolific of the monkey salesmen of Victorian London was Charles Jamrach, whose shop in East London was a half-hour omnibus ride from the Seven Dials area where Carr often walked to see the birds offered for sale in cages.[39] Jamrach's Wild Beast Mart was captured in an illustration published in the *Daily News* in 1873. Under the rafters of a warehouse loft, we see closely stacked boxes with caged fronts containing animals as diverse as mongooses, a baboon, an anteater and some form of wild cat, while a cockatoo sits near a small wood stove, eying the resident warehouse feline sitting atop a tiny cage containing a frightened animal hiding in the back.[40]

Is it that simple, then? Is that how Carr came to be in Mrs. Cowie's shop that day, for more self-imposed exposure therapy? "When my fear of monkeys went," Carr wrote, "my fear of darkness went also."[41]

On that day in 1923, what Carr saw in the barrel at Lucy Cowie's shop was "a pathetic little face" with "surprised Kewpie hair" that stood up between two elfin ears. This monkey's expression haunted her, even as it kept disappearing beneath the scrambling feet and curling tails of the larger, stronger ones. Mrs. Cowie recommended the monkey to Carr, evidently seeing in her anxious features the chance of an easy sale. "The big ones bully her," she warned, expertly pulling on her heart strings. Mrs. Cowie didn't have to work very hard to convince Carr to make a decision. "Suddenly I wanted her—I wanted her *tremendously*," Carr wrote years later in words brimming with emotion.[42] Though pet stores are not often places of rescue but exchange of goods for cash, it's clear that in Carr's heart, this transaction was the former. Someone had to save this baby monkey, and that someone was her.

Even rescue comes at a price. Carr blanched when Mrs. Cowie told her that the monkey would set her back thirty dollars. Carr didn't have cash like that simply lying around the house. She was then a decade into her ill-fitting, and ill-rewarding, day job as landlady of the two-storey apartment house at 646 Simcoe Street she had built on family land in 1913. But the venture was anything but a carefree provider of dividends. Soon after opening for business, Carr began to have regular altercations with tenants who, according to her, appear to have been unusually difficult characters, placing her in a perpetual daily cycle of anger, recrimination and some remorse, for she could not exist without them, and the shred of her ladylike upbringing that remained shrank from the possibility that she had turned into a shrew. (It should be noted that Carr evidently could be an especially fearsome landlady: her friend the artist Edythe Hembroff-Schleicher recalled how the common bathroom on the apartment house's second storey was veritably papered with notes covered in Carr's rapid scrawl, each sentence ending with an exclamation mark: "Don't throw matches in the toilet!" "Don't use Draino!")[43] In the years during and after World War I, rents had fallen sharply. Carr found she had to lease out her own quarters in the building and set up a tent in the garden for herself, then move into an attic, just to make ends meet, making a mockery of her original rosy plans. "Everything together only brought in what a flat and a half had before the war," Carr wrote.[44] In the meantime, for some years to follow, very little painting got done. (She was not alone. Group of Seven member A.Y. Jackson would comment that there had never been more disinterest in painting in Canada than in the years following the war.) This only increased Carr's daily frustrations as her dreams remained becalmed.[45]

Standing in Lucy Cowie's shop, the air laced with bird calls and parrot squawks, puppy barks and monkey chatter, and faced with a price for a monkey she certainly did not need, at a cost she could not afford, but which her heart told her she absolutely had to have, Carr at length told Mrs. Cowie she had to go home and think about it. Before letting her depart, Mrs. Cowie, who seems to have combined the skill of the saleswoman with the coaxing genius of a former lady's maid, sweetened the deal: if Carr would be willing to add one of the dogs from her prized Brussels griffon kennels, the balance owing would just be a few dollars cash.

Carr took this information under advisement. When she got home to Simcoe Street, she spoke about the kewpie-faced monkey to her maid, whom she called Pearl. Though Carr was by no means affluent she, like many people in her circumstances in the years before appropriate living wages for household help became the norm, was able to afford a servant. Carr was a self-possessed person, but a part of her never stopped being the youngest sister in a family of elder ones who constantly told her what to do and what to think. Having been brought up from the cradle surrounded by accommodating and supportive servants, she never got out of the habit of leaning on them as needed. Pearl, also an animal lover, was delighted to hear that her employer was seriously considering bringing a monkey into the house, and offered to fetch her from the Bird and Pet Shop. There was likely never any question that Carr would buy the monkey, yet Pearl's enthusiasm clearly tipped the scales in that direction. And, after all, as Carr herself would write, "Inspiration is intention obeyed." Thus it is Pearl we have to thank for running downtown and bringing Woo home, penned in the temporary transport device of a hastily grabbed birdcage.[46]

Pearl had not been away for long when Carr, seated at lunch with guests in her second-floor studio, heard footsteps on the stairs and a persistent wail—"woo ... woo"—that drew nearer. With Emily at the table were her sister, Elizabeth Carr, called Lizzie, and a male boarder. Lizzie, born in 1867, was only four years older than Emily but seemed much the senior by virtue of her passionate devotion to an especially arid variety of Christianity and her inheritance of authority over Emily on the death, in 1919, of their disciplinary sister Edith, Emily's elder by fifteen years. It can truly be said that if Emily's eyes were focused on the sublime artistry of Nature, Lizzie's were set with Dickensian "telescopic philanthropy" on African villages full of men, women and children awaiting Christian grace at her hands. Because her dreams of bringing salvation to exotic climes were unrealized, Lizzie turned her telescopic energies toward organizing prayer circles closer to home, serving as missionary to Indigenous peoples on the coast of British Columbia.

Lizzie was straight of back, kind but cool of expression, and no lover of Emily's menagerie—to her Victorian mind, these were creatures that had escaped the proper confines of a zoo. All three faces turned to see the smiling housemaid standing in the doorway, and in the cage hanging from her hand two bright eyes and an active body. Over and over again, the monkey continued to give out the same plaintive vocalization—"woo."[47]

Emily turned to Lizzie, sitting open-mouthed, and said, "Your new niece, Lizzie!" Pushing her plate away, Lizzie spluttered, "I never thought a relative of mine would sink to a baboon!"[48]

Monkeys were definitely not Lizzie's cup of tea, but she regained her composure sufficiently, and her authority as head of the house of Carr, to demand how much the monkey had cost. Emily's allegedly spendthrift ways had a long tradition of chastisement in the family, part of the Carr women's apparent view that their sister was incapable of rational adult behaviour. One would have thought, wrote Carr, that she had traded diamonds for an apple. On being told that her sister had struck a bargain with Lucy Cowie, using one of her griffons to cover the balance, Lizzie—who didn't much care for Emily's dogs either—continued to remonstrate with her sister, going on to enumerate the other consequences that would befall her thanks to this monkey. The house would smell. The monkey would break everything in sight. Carr would find that because of all these monkey-induced disasters, she would soon have no friends. In a small, highly stratified society like that of Victoria, lack of friends was not to be sniffed at. Did she want to be shunned in public, in church? Did she wish to lose the tenants she had and the income they generated for her? (This warning was predictable: as

Carr wrote, her sisters were "always siding with the tenant."[49]) To each of these issues, Carr had a response; and while the discussion raged, the monkey began to take matters in her own hands. "Sticking one hand and one foot out of each side of the narrow cage," Carr wrote, "she propelled herself across the floor," as if the cage had suddenly sprouted limbs and was walking of its own accord.[50] Whatever the outcome of the human argument around the table, the monkey had clearly decided that this was home.

That same day, Alice, the sister closest to Carr in age, who dwelt on a piece of family land around the corner from the apartment house, mounted the stairs to Carr's studio. After taking an appraising look, she greeted the monkey with caution and her special brand of genteel disapproval. "Everyone to his own taste," she said dismissively.[51] Alice would make this attitude very clear in years to come, at a time when she, rather than Emily, held ultimate authority over this monkey's fate.

Though Emily's sisters could push all her buttons, frequently leaving her to stew over some careless remark about her art or her animals, she was able to tolerate a judgement that, in the end, was no surprise to her. Though Lizzie and Alice had had pets in childhood and a few later on, and were supportive of the work of the Society for the Prevention of Cruelty to Animals, it was the sheer number and variety of Carr's animal family that concerned them, rather than any dislike of animals per se. Had Carr stuck with a few cats and dogs, or run her kennels in a more professional manner (according to Lizzie's and Alice's ideals of professionalism), and not paraded her pets on shopping trips in downtown Victoria, all might have been well and good. Carr was aware of this scorn and, aside from some annoyance, was able to discount her sisters' disapprobation, little realizing how large it would loom when poor health would eventually rob Carr of control over her animals and what happened to them.

Carr's tenants, however, were another matter entirely. Would they accept living under the same roof as a monkey? One tenant, an elderly lady, on later meeting Carr's monkey, would ominously recount the tale of King Alexander of Greece, who had died in 1920 at age twenty-seven from an infected monkey bite.[52] This was just the sort of anecdote that, fuelled by foreign tabloids and spreading among the other residents, could cause more trouble than Lizzie's and Alice's disapproval put together, simply because everyone wanted to believe the worst where a monkey was concerned.

After everyone departed that day the monkey arrived on Simcoe Street, Carr and Pearl were left in the studio with the animal, still shifting her cage across the floor. Both women wondered what to make of what Carr called "a jungle stranger"—a guest with whom they did not at first know what to do. There was no doubt in Carr's mind, however, that she had made the right decision in bringing the monkey home. Though Carr had the initial unprepossessing impression that the monkey "ungraciously" grabbed at whatever food was offered her, the creature soon became attached to the artist and her animal-loving maid.[53] After all, from the monkey's perspective, a female primate had released her from her crate, another female primate had brought her away from the Bird and Pet Shop to this house, and now yet another female primate, whose dominant personality she surely must have sensed and perhaps welcomed, stood over her protectively.

Perhaps it seemed to the monkey that she had come full circle, back to the feminine family structure from which she had been torn. In Carr, that feminine, maternal sensibility was, in turn, activated by the monkey's special needs. In the coming years, Carr would be constantly worried about whether the monkey was warm enough. Born into a tropical climate, she now lived in windy James Bay. Pearl offered an idea—to take off her sweater and put it in the cage with the monkey. Wrapped around a heated brick, the warmed sweater smelled of the woman who had rescued the little monkey from the chaos and bullying of Lucy Cowie's store. Of course it would comfort her to be reminded of Pearl. So, rolling herself up in the sweater, and with the warmth of the brick against her small body, the monkey quietened, and finally slept, and Carr and Pearl were able to go about the tasks of their day, pondering as they did so what to call her.[54] She had to be called something, after all. "Every creature accepting domesticity is entitled to a name," Carr wrote, as if delivering a royal decree.[55] In the end, it was the monkey's very vocal longing, expressed in her plaintive "woo," that provided an answer.

Carr noted that her original intention was to call the monkey Jemima—a biblical name meaning "little dove." It should also be acknowledged that this name had long been associated with a certain stereotype of black women in the American South, a kind of stock figure in minstrel shows, soon to appear on boxes of pancake mix. Given that Carr had a confessed preference for naming her male bobtail sheepdogs after Old Testament patriarchs, this is perhaps where the name had its origin. Remove the ugly racial associations, and there would have been a lovely biblical symbolism in the name. After all, in the Book of Job, Jemima was one of the three beautiful daughters of that much put-upon man, born to Job when his luck turned to the better. Perhaps Carr saw the monkey as a lucky charm when she most felt, as artist and woman, that she was perpetually on the receiving end of misfortune.

That first day when, from upstairs in her attic bedroom, Carr heard the "jungle stranger" crying from her cage in the studio, in a plaintive wail like the call of an owl in the night, she hurried down to comfort her, echoing her cry, which was echoed back to her in turn. "Woo" became their first shared communication. And that cry, "woo ... woo," not Jemima, became the monkey's name. And what better name than one homonymous with that Old English word whose definition, "to bend or incline (some)one toward oneself," could not have been more apt, in years to come, for the relationship between monkey and artist.

In time, it would be a key to a large part of Carr's own fame. Woo the jungle creature offered what Carr termed a "foreign, undomestic note" in a setting she considered drab and workaday. The monkey also brought a ray of light to dispel a darkness Carr no longer needed to fear—a light which, in truth, her painter's brush and writer's pen had long been seeking, like an animal pacing in its cage, and at last let out the door.[56] Perhaps, too, Carr had attained at last a version of the privileged state she revered and missed, "the stupendous wholeness" of motherhood. It must be, she wrote, "an enormous lesson in mellowing."[57] For Carr the woman and Carr the artist, it was a mellowing that would make all the difference.

CHAPTER 3

"An Artist's Queer Equipment"

The animals who were Carr's lodestone for unadulterated love were also part of her enduring reputation as a quirky spinster, a legend fed by local gossip and her own preference for the company of animals over that of her own kind.

Even at her greatest extremity of mental and physical health, during a year spent in an English sanatorium after she had suffered a nervous breakdown in 1903, the thirty-two-year-old artist had managed to find interest in and strength for taming and breeding wild birds. In the process, what seemed to help heal her spirit provided similar therapy to her fellow patients, some of them living their last days. "Common boredom, common interests, knit us tight," Carr said, recalling keen efforts by the other patients to gather food for the nestlings.[58]

That said, other people, even helpful ones, were never more than supporting players in Carr's lifelong drama starring herself and animals. She had known this since asking for the first live animal she ever had for her own. She would be his god, the young Carr said of the canary she was given as a very young girl.[59] This isn't to say Carr didn't see animals as having godlike powers themselves. But as the reference to a deity implies, Carr's love for animals had something in it of the sublime, at best, and of the selective possessiveness of a collector of art or rare books, at worst. "Just to touch wild things made me crazy happy," Carr would confess.[60] She had not only to touch them; she had to possess them, often without regard to practicality or, most critically, to the ethics of whether she should be holding a "wild thing" in her hands in the first place. What makes this passion even more strange is that Carr habitually accorded natural laws the upper hand in all her dealings with animals, letting nature take its course—except where her own human intervention, called upon at her discretion, was concerned, not always improving their situation.

Did this have something to do with the fact that so many of the animals from Carr's youth had been taken from her, or that the continuation of their presence in her life was held in the balance as a punitive measure? Her very first puppy, given to her as a little girl, is a case in point. This pet, whom Carr named Tibby, was to be hers for only a short time. Deemed dangerous by Carr's eldest sister Edith, after a couple of occasions when the dog was provoked to the point where he nipped the people who were teasing him, Tibby was put down. Significantly, this took place at Edith's request when Emily was too incapacitated in bed with a childhood malady to do anything about it—foreshadowing another occasion, decades later, when another sister would dispose of Carr's animals while she, recovering from a heart attack, was in no position to intervene.[61]

Tibby was only the first of a long line of animal family for whom Carr clearly felt more of an affinity than for the humans around her, which her disapproving sisters, from Edith to Lizzie to Alice, refused to take seriously and saw as proof of their youngest sister's inability to join the ranks of mature, orderly, devout women they and their prayer-circle friends considered themselves to be.[62] Which is why, when Woo came into the picture, it seemed to ladies of this highly judgemental mould that Carr had completely gone off the deep end.

Despite the fact that Carr's sisters and their circle of friends were scandalized by the arrival of Woo, monkeys kept as pets were by no means unusual just about anywhere in the world. Lucy Cowie apparently sold them with enough regularity and profit to go on importing them (so long as this remained legal under the British law that governed Canada). As Carr would have known, monkeys were common enough in the France where she had studied in 1910–12: Georges Seurat's revolutionary pointillist work *Sunday Afternoon on the Island of La Grande Jatte*, depicting a scene of middle-class leisure activity in 1880s Paris, includes a monkey frolicking in the foreground with dogs, as if nothing were more normal. Even in the remote British Empire enclave of Victoria, monkeys were part of the landscape. Long before the Bird and Pet Shop came into existence, Beacon Hill Park Zoo, dating from 1889, when Carr was in her late teens, included monkeys among its many other animal exhibits. And we know hotelier Mrs. Lush had allowed her monkeys to wander pretty much at will through the neighbourhood and into people's houses until the authorities stepped in.[63] But even for Carr, a monkey took some getting used to, not least in terms of learning to deal with a personality that in many respects mirrored her own, which was no more amenable to control. "Monkey tempers are inflammable," Carr wrote. "So is mine."[64]

Carr was indulging in a certain primate stereotype, one to which wise monkey people like Lucy Cowie's friend Lilian M. Russell knew better than to give too much credence. As a child of Victorian England, Russell had travelled with her parents through exotic places seen by few English children, and brought back, as she wrote, "all kinds of creatures" to her parents' home in the Kensington suburb of London, including a scorpion and an alligator. But she immediately ran into problems when she acquired a monkey. Russell's mother declared that the creature would destroy everything around her. It looked for a moment as if she was correct. Called Kawa after the White Nile village where she was bought, true to the dire predictions of Russell's mother, the monkey proceeded to run helter-skelter about the family's tall London house. Yet even Russell's mother had to admit that the hyperkinetic Kawa, "threading her way through labyrinths of china vases, elaborate clocks, candlesticks and various Victorian superfluities as harmlessly as a small kitten," was able to do so without breaking anything at all. She had an inborn agile grace that protected her from damaging her surroundings. She even leaped into a hot fireplace and survived. Like Kawa, Woo would handle fragile objects with the utmost delicacy.

Like Woo, Kawa would direct all her love toward a dog. Like Woo, Kawa would ingest poisonous substances in what may have been bids for attention and, like Woo, would somehow survive her own curiosity. And like Woo, house-bred Kawa would spend her final months of life in the controlled isolation of a cage.[65]

Temperamental as Woo could be, she—like Carr—was nevertheless always a "lady," according to Carr. As the flip side to Woo's irascibility, Carr would come to see in the monkey a delicacy, a respect for rules as she understood them, a refinement even, that went against the common perception, as conveyed by Carr's sisters, that a monkey would bring the house down around Carr's head (and which, again, mirrored their fixed critical impression of Carr herself). This delicacy extended to the human bric-a-brac that Kawa, too, had handled with such gracefulness. Carr's friend Carol Pearson, one of Carr's drawing students, described once watching Woo empty teacups of their sugary dregs when she thought she was not being observed. "Her little brown hands were no more than two inches long," Pearson recalled, "yet you have never handled your own Dresden china with more care."[66] Woo, who had a delicacy of manner as well as of action, would put this delicacy to the test in an encounter that might well have turned tragic.

The first problem Woo had to grapple with was getting to know Carr's other animals, especially her dogs. There is always a period of adjustment when a new animal joins those who were there first. Woo had likely never met a dog, other than brief encounters with those offered for sale in Lucy Cowie's shop. Carr was careful to introduce Woo to her griffons not indoors but out under the open sky, in the garden back of the house, where there were cherry and apple trees, flowers and fruit and a multi-trunked cedar shaped like a sort of arboreal basket. "Then [Woo] saw the earth and scrambled down in an ecstasy of joy, feeling, smelling, tasting the delight of soil and grass after cage confinement! She turned the stones over and found earwigs and beetles, crunching them with keen relish."[67]

Carr made sure Woo was fastened to a chain for this maiden outing. (Carol Pearson would later note with astonishment that even though Woo disliked the chain and knew how to disengage herself from it, "it was amazing how seldom she took advantage and released herself."[68]) Though she never cared for it, finding all sorts of ways to escape it, Woo most definitely appreciated the chain the first day she met Carr's dogs. When the diminutive griffon dogs, with their flat noses, bearded chins and pronounced underbite, rushed at the monkey, Carr hoisted her up by her leash, high above the scruffy barking snouts. "Woo scrambled to my shoulder screeching," Carr wrote. As the dogs jumped, Woo held on to Carr's shirt collar with her prehensile toes, lowering herself to slap at the eager bodies vaulting up at her from the grass.[69]

When the dogs, having lost interest in the monkey, began to play among themselves on the grass, Carr let Woo down, and the monkey sat and watched them. One griffon ran past her, and with a swiftness that startled both Carr and the dog, Woo grasped its tail, refusing to let go. Brussels griffons were bred for use much after the pattern of terriers, to control rodent populations on farms. Thus a fearless scrappiness was bred into their character. And like many small dogs, their sense of self is in direct disproportion to their physical size; they will take on a larger dog—or monkey—if they feel threatened. But Woo grabbed the right griffon. Ginger Pop, as Carr had named him, was the jewel of Carr's griffon treasure. He could be so quiet it was as if he were not even in the room, but when he saw the preparations for a journey with Carr, he could scarcely keep inside his box en route, eyes shining fitfully. Faithful, affectionate, possessive, Ginger was ever-present wherever Carr was; Carol Pearson related how, years after he had died, Carr, confined to bed with heart trouble, would still absently drop a hand down beside as if expecting the tousled head to be waiting there for a friendly scruff.[70]

Ginger Pop, who was not a great deal larger than the monkey, allowed Woo to pull him toward her, and even then did not object when she spun him around to face her, holding him tightly by his fluffy cheeks. "Levelling her eyes to his," Carr wrote, "Woo stared straight into them, mouth open, eyes glaring." This is not behaviour with which most dogs—or primates—are comfortable. There are typically five reasons why a dog will meet another animal's stare without turning away: affection, curiosity, interest in what the animal has, an attempt to convey a need or aggression. Most dog experts warn parents not to let their children go eye to eye with a strange dog, as the animal's stare may be based in aggression and could lead to injury if the child provokes it. In this instance, it was Woo who displayed aggression, and Woo who could have injured the dog had she so chosen. Ginger Pop, his face held firmly in Woo's hands, did not struggle to escape. His golden eyes looked into hers and, in so doing, seemed to calm her. Carr watched as Woo released her grip. She saw Ginger Pop sit down beside Woo, where he allowed her to groom his ginger coat. "From that day on," wrote Carr, "he and Woo were inseparable companions." They played together, she noted, like two dogs—or two monkeys.[71] (It is interesting to speculate whether Carr saw a monkey as a being midpoint between dog and human—a furry and playful creature, like a dog, with hands and feet, just human enough yet refreshingly canine.)

Meanwhile, another Woo-related challenge lay in that always more complex area of human dynamics: the management of Carr's tenants. Carr's suite in Hill House was located on the building's second floor, on the east side facing Beacon Hill Park, with two steep flights of steps up from her secluded garden at the back to access it. Carr had designed the building with specific instructions to safeguard her own privacy from the lives of those to whom she rented units. So it should not have been difficult keeping Woo away from her tenants' prying eyes. But whatever Carr's efforts to keep Woo on the down-low, word had spread through Hill House that a monkey had come to reside under their mutual roof. Responses were what Carr had expected. One woman opined that Woo would soon turn everything in the house upside down, making a perfect wreck of things. Another tenant claimed she would make too much noise (a comment that must have moved Carr, who so often endured noisy arguments and assorted auditory annoyances from her tenants, to roll her eyes). And another resident noted there would always be the danger of monkey bites that, after all, had even killed a king. One tenant sniffed, "It will smell," though in truth, Carr could tell her a thing or two about her olfactory sufferings on that score from her human tenants. "Being a landlady was never agreeable to me," Carr sighed, so she, as sure of pushback from tenants as from her sisters, was not at all surprised.[72] Yet the tide did turn, sooner than the sceptical Carr would herself have believed. "Soon people accepted Woo as part of an artist's queer equipment," Carr wrote, glorying in *vive la différence*.[73]

Afraid that Woo might suffer during winter in a climate so completely different from that of her Javanese place of origin, Carr put Woo to bed at night in the basement, where the furnace kept the area and Woo constantly warm. "A house's underneathness is crushing," Carr wrote of this confined space.[74] Yet it could be said that very coziness may have given Woo a sense of security. More than a crawl space but impossible to navigate standing upright, Hill House's basement was only partly underground, with windows on three sides and two exit doors. Not completely finished, the basement had dirt floors.[75] It had no interior entrance from the house and could only be accessed from the garden or from the east side of the building. The latter door was used primarily for coal deliveries, which Woo both enjoyed and feared, according to Carr. In Carr's account of one of the coal man's regular visits, once "the wind rolls in the open window," Woo runs to her sleeping box and pulls the blanket over her head; but as the sack "thunders its contents into the bin, she draws aside her covers and peeps."[76] Even in winter, the basement was quite warm, with the combination of heat from the house above, the coal furnace below (next to which Woo's bed was placed), and sun from the windows. This was the perfect atmosphere for an animal with the heat of tropical climes in her blood, but living in the basement left Woo by herself a good deal of the time. Her reaction to isolation makes it clear that she did not enjoy it, and modern research shows that isolation for any length of time is harmful to a monkey's well-being. In a 2009 study, the authors noted how primates situated in the wild spent almost half their time foraging for food, and only about 10 to 30 per cent of their time at rest. It is easy to see why primates kept in domestic settings, in which they are caged most of the time and when released briefly are still trapped inside four walls and a ceiling, would be frustrated physically and mentally by their confinement.[77] Later on in Woo's life story, as we see her instances of acting out in self-harmful ways and in aggression toward strangers, the consequences of having to live a primate's life on human terms are all too obvious.

Carr was pleasantly surprised to find, when she was called away on errands, that some of her tenants were willing to step in to help the monkey—proving that whatever the general unease at her presence at Hill House, not all the residents were afraid of Woo. One night, while Carr was away for a few hours, an elderly lady tenant, having been awakened by Woo's cries, made her way downstairs in the dark to comfort her, staying with her until Carr returned. On another occasion, Carr had to go out of town for the day. She had left Woo amply provided for in the basement, but the monkey, not unnaturally frightened and confused at being alone, had cried for her. On her return, Carr discovered that another tenant had heard Woo's distress and had come down to spend most of the day sitting with her on the woodpile adjacent to her sleeping box, keeping her company. Soon the ladies of Hill House went further. Finding that Woo enjoyed sweet things like cherries, grapes and candy, they made sure to bring her some regularly. When it was discovered that Woo liked looking at her reflection, gazing into a mirror for hours at a time, they donated small looking glasses for her use. "Woo sat holding the hand mirror with her feet," remembered Carr, "and her hands felt behind for the other monkey and her lips kissed and kissed."[78] By these means, Carr wrote, "Woo wove herself into the atmosphere of 646 Simcoe Street, accepting attention with regal indifference." And Carr would learn, through their interactions with this simian resident, that her tenants were not all bad—a significant lesson in her case.[79]

Woo's mysteriously attractive regal indifference began to draw the notice of the world outside Hill House too. Carr's basement windows, three in a row, could be seen by anyone descending Simcoe Street from Beacon Hill Park. There, on the sills, Woo was so often spied warming herself in the winter sun that Carr began to hear that pedestrians passing in the street were going out of their way in order to enjoy the privilege of seeing the monkey crouching in the window. These sightings became so important to the general public in the neighbourhood that people began to express concern when Woo was suddenly no longer to be seen in the window. Neighbours asked Carr, with wide, concerned eyes, "Is the monkey dead?" She laughed. Very much to the contrary, she said, Woo was very much alive—she was occupying her summer quarters in the back garden, a wooden box that Carr, who wielded a mean hammer, had nailed into the crook of a cherry tree.[80] This now-you-see-her-now-you-don't aspect, so like the tricks employed by the vaudeville magicians of the time, only heightened Woo's mystique, as nobody but Carr's friends gained access to the garden and then only infrequently.

Part of Woo's attraction, of course, was her clothing. Monkeys wearing costumes were a commonplace thing for those who had been to see the circus or vaudeville entertainments, but those wearing clothes were probably not too often to be seen in Victoria's private homes. Carr's reason for putting them on Woo was a solidly practical one. Victoria has chill winters and cool springs, and summer days can unexpectedly turn cold when winds whip up off Juan de Fuca Strait. Soon after Woo arrived at Hill House, Carr began to sew simple canvas dresses to keep her warm. Carr had originally dressed the shivering monkey in a flannel gown; when she tore it into pieces, Carr resolved to use tougher fabric. Pearl had another practical idea to recommend. Make the skirts wider, she told Carr. It would be like giving a little girl plenty of room to run in her dress, and Woo clearly felt hemmed in by the original clothes Carr had made for her, hence her strenuous efforts to escape from them. The new version of the outfit was similarly destroyed when Woo discovered how to remove the buttons that fastened it in back. Carr persisted and, finally, by using buckles at the back and the neck, found a way to keep Woo's clothes on her despite her best Houdini escape efforts.[81] Carr doesn't mention it, but her friend Carol Pearson recalled how she originally stitched Woo into her dresses, up the back, where she couldn't reach, adding a pocket ("which had had to be nearly welded on!" Pearson stated), into which Carr placed a candy each time Woo stopped tugging at the garment. Once Woo realized that it was to her benefit to accept the pinafore, she resigned herself to her garment, and Carr was able to sew buttons up the back again. The result—more dress, less straitjacket—surely was an improvement for Woo.[82]

Carr would paint a portrait of Woo wearing a very different garment from this, but the entire image is suffused with more ideal than real. In the painting, Woo stands on a tree branch, toes curled around its bark as she holds herself upright using a branch higher up. She gazes away from the observer at an expanse of blue sky, seemingly less a monkey longing for freedom from her chain, more like a little girl looking over the fence into the mysteries of a neighbour's garden. She is wearing a proper dress of orange fabric, the wide skirt edged with a red stripe and the waist tied at the back with a yellow ribbon. Perhaps this is an early version of the garment Carr eventually found workable for Woo, the one that got torn to bits, or Carr has taken artistic licence to improve the smock Woo customarily wore. Yet looking at this Woo, one could scarcely imagine her causing any such havoc, as she intently surveys life outside the picture's frame. Perhaps she is on her best behaviour for Carr's sisters, coming up the sidewalk from their respective residences nearby.

Emily, Lizzie and Alice lived only a few minutes' walk away from each other. Each had taken a parcel of their father's land in James Bay after his death, and each had built on their plot a place to live and to do business. Given this proximity, the sisters formed a habit of visiting one another's houses in the evening, weather permitting. "Each had her own house, interests, friends," Carr pointed out—indeed, as close as they lived to one another, in terms of interests and personalities, each could have been on a separate planet. Like Lavinia Dickinson, sister of poet Emily, who wrote of her own family in remote Amherst, Massachusetts, that they "lived like friendly and absolute monarchs, each in his own domain,"[83] the Carr sisters lived apart, like queens regnant over slices of a joint territory. Through sentimental memories, cherished by Victorians the world over, and through the bonds of love that stitched tight and held together a family for reasons none can explain but all dutifully accept, they formed a unity of blood and shared experience that overrode—most of the time—their obvious differences, which in the case of these three sisters were more obvious from Lizzie's and Alice's standpoint when they looked at their younger sister. On Emily's part, there was the overarching sense of obedience to her elder sisters, and of duty, which even in this rebel was strong enough to keep her from living a life of complete personal freedom. So, though Emily knew that a visit to her sisters was apt to include criticism of some aspect of her life, she went regularly anyway, always accompanied by her animal family—"a taggle of dogs, a Persian cat, and the monkey"—as if taking reinforcements into battle.[84]

These two older sisters followed similar occupations, both of which involved service to others. Alice kept a school for children, many of them quite young. They slept, ate and were taught their letters in a schoolroom under Alice's roof. Lizzie's physical therapy work typically meant she had to go to where her clients lived, as many were elderly and frail. It was this obdurate industriousness that blinkered them to their sister's labours in the fields of art and prodded Carr, in turn, to prove herself to them by readily assuming the responsibilities for cleaning, repairs and general labour required by her apartment house. Carr worked just as hard to get Lizzie and Alice to accept Woo as she did to seek their approbation for her work as artist.[85]

Woo herself did not help matters much, because she seemed bent on doing everything she could to make Carr's sisters dislike her. For example, it was not unusual, on Carr's arrival at Alice's home, for her to find her sister up to her elbows in suds bathing children in her small kitchen. With Carr and even a few animals, plus the children, this made for a tight squeeze in the tiny room, and Woo did nothing to improve this, taking advantage of the confusion to steal soap from the tub, or try to drink the bathwater, or by filching a washcloth to shred with her sharp teeth.[86] Lizzie dwelt in a very different setting. Her living room was lined with piously displayed, regularly situated framed prayers and moral admonitions, along with photographs of missionaries in action, "dashing up raging rivers in war canoes," as Carr described, "to dispense Epsom salts and hymn books to Indians."[87] Woo plunged into this solemn setting like a firecracker in a graveyard. She appeared to enjoy rushing straight up to Lizzie's taciturn missionary and prayer circle visitors in an effort to reach the warm hearth, unmindful of the humans gathered there. Seeing her scamper across the carpet toward them, the ladies would scatter, lifting their skirts and squealing, while the men gazed heavenward, murmuring unheard prayers (or curses).[88]

But the sisters did begin to thaw toward Woo, and if they did not ever really approve of or even like her, they did recognize and depend on her usefulness. Before long, wrote Carr, Alice began to incorporate Woo into her lessons, in the form of stories, on those occasions when Woo was not physically there to dazzle the children. She and her pupils started a yearly tradition by filling a Christmas stocking just for Woo and watching with glee as the monkey did not reach inside for her treats but chewed open portions of the stocking where she knew the candies and fruits were, with none of the respect or decorum those same children were expected to show toward their own stockings on so solemn an occasion. And unlike them, Woo was allowed to discard all such silly human etiquette associated with receiving gifts. When she did not care for what she found in her shredded stocking, Woo simply threw it aside "with a grunt of scorn," much to the sympathetic delight of the children.[89] Woo's freedom to do whatever she felt like doing provided a vicarious thrill in a world of man-made restrictions on all-too-human behavioural urges.

Woo served a similarly beneficial role for Lizzie. As a physical therapist who worked mostly with geriatric clientele, Lizzie was often either chatting volubly with or bearing up in the silence of a nervous, querulous or pain-ridden patient as she massaged their limbs. Over time, wrote Carr, Lizzie began to realize that by relating stories about Woo's latest adventures to her patients, they seemed to perk up and derive more satisfaction and benefit from the treatments because they were relaxed. Thanks to Woo, Lizzie was able "to win a smile from some weary bedridden old soul who had nothing but a ceiling to look at and no fun in her mind at all."[90]

At Lizzie's prompting, Carr began to take Woo with her to visit elderly shut-ins on her sister's client list. Woo never failed to cheer them, at the same time serving as ambassador of goodwill on behalf of her fellow primates for those people conditioned to see monkeys as agents of the devil or murderers of Greek monarchs. In effect, Lizzie, as part of a medical tradition reaching at least as far back as Florence Nightingale, recognized the calming and healing power of an animal on a sick or injured person. "A small animal is often an excellent companion for the sick," wrote Nightingale, noting that an animal was often judged the better caregiver: "An invalid, in giving an account of his nursing by a nurse and a dog, infinitely preferred that of the dog."[91] This method was not to go into general use until the late twentieth and early twenty-first centuries, and is still not fully accepted in mainstream medicine even now.

But even without all this, Carr well knew what a gem she had at the end of Woo's chain. "Unsuspecting little Woo had a place to fill," Carr wrote, "and a part to play in the big thing called life."[92] And Woo would play a part in the big development that was about to happen to her artist "mother."

CHAPTER 4

No Man's Land

With an age difference between them of thirty-six years, and birthplaces—Mexico City and Victoria—that could not be more different, Frida Kahlo and Emily Carr shared one important similarity beyond the fact that they were artists: an affinity for animals essential to their creativity.

Indeed, like Carr, Kahlo seemed to need them as balm for wounds that, in her case, were of both body and soul. And she felt a special affection for monkeys, which she took to be protective entities, painting herself surrounded by them—peeping out of jungle foliage behind her, cradled in her arms. The relationship was actually more complicated than her paintings suggest. If they protected her, she also was their protector. In her 1943 *Self-Portrait with Monkeys*, Kahlo poses almost belligerently, stiff in her white blouse, while the four monkeys around her gaze with apprehension toward something other than what Kahlo is focused on—as if she were getting so lost in her vigilance she was unable to comprehend the real dangers that lay all around her. If she is their vigilant mother, they are her worried children. But to shield them from harm, she will take on an army to defend her simian progeny who, as Kahlo's paintings seem to suggest, served as an escape valve through which she could indulge in vicarious comedy. Perhaps art historian Sharyn Rohlfsen Udall put it best: "[Kahlo's] sense of humor, often earthy and ribald, was tickled by the antics of the monkeys, whose uninhibited behaviour exceeded what humans were permitted," even a free spirit like Kahlo.[93] There are no photographs of Emily Carr with any of her animals where she looks to be in anything but an exuberant mood, a state of being in which she did not often find herself. But then, for Carr as for Kahlo, animals were heaven.

No one would take a monkey into her life thinking she would tame it like a well-behaved human child. Along with the instinct to mother this human-like being is that instinct that itself comes from childhood, to revel in the behaviour of a creature who does whatever it pleases with very few if any consequences, protected by its charm. For Carr, with her crippling self-consciousness, her knee-jerk distrust of everyone and equally painful doubts about herself, Woo did all this and more: she became Carr's guide into a part of her self which, like the forests of British Columbia, she had to visit in order to become all the artist she was meant to be. This brought her to a place of freedom and fearlessness, "a no man's land," Carr wrote, "where beast and human meet."[94] Dr. Jane Goodall recently described, speaking of the early period in her study of the social lives of chimpanzees, her view that though science and religion both seemed busy finding ways to prove that primates and humans were different, study of the ways of primates proved that far from establishing defined boundaries of difference, there were many more areas where primates and humans intersected and overlapped.[95] That common ground between Woo and Carr became a powerful leverage for creativity, as well as for love, for both human and monkey, without judgement or fear.

Kahlo knew not to treat a companion animal as a kind of human being in a dog, cat or monkey costume, but as a discrete individual of innate selfhood deserving of respect and dignity for being just who and what it is. Like Kahlo, Carr also disapproved of anthropomorphism. When it was suggested by a friend that she write about her animal family from their point of view, putting words in the mouths of Dolf the cat or Koko the dog, she was characteristically abrupt in her response: "That's twaddle."[96] In Carr's view, animals just needed to be allowed to *be*—to exist in their reality unaltered by human expectation or imagination. "In their mute unworded way, they must despise us and our patronizing," Carr wrote in her journal (ironically, putting thoughts in her animals' heads).[97] We can guess whether Carr's opinion was in some way also informed by her distrust of art critics and fear of the critical gaze of the public—also too often patronizing, often not letting her just *be*.

Carr knew before she brought Woo into her life that an animal lives in the moment, not in the past (though it can be argued that past experiences, particularly when they involve trauma, do a lot to shape an animal's response to the present, as they do with humans). And once Carr learned how to live in that same moment, going neither backward nor forward in time but dwelling in the now, she grew as a person and, especially important, she grew as an artist. And in my view, that growth had a lot to do with changes Woo brought into Carr's life—above all, her decision to relinquish a burden that had been blocking her from fully leveraging her art and her vision to share both with the wider world. It's a burden that has blocked artists—poets, painters, musicians, dancers—since time began: that sharp, single-syllable word, fear.

Emily Carr had been working at her craft for a very long time. Starting with drawings made in childhood (one of which, a portrait of the family dog sketched in charcoal, earned the approbation of Richard Carr, who supported Emily's interest in art), Carr had doggedly pursued a formal art education. From 1890 to 1893, she studied in San Francisco. From 1899 to 1904, she studied in England, and from 1910 to 1912 in France. She had lived and taught in Vancouver (from 1906 to 1910), where her frank personality and bold style rubbed some people the wrong way. She rubbed some in Victoria the wrong way too. The provincial capital's small, insular artistic circles, strung on sturdy threads of conservatism, preferred pretty, bland watercolours; it saw a "lady artist" as defined by a woman of good family who brushed roses and violets on china, to be entered in the agricultural fair alongside her preserves. "Misty landscapes and gentle cows do not express Western Canada," Carr told a no doubt astonished Victoria audience in remarks delivered before her 1930 one-woman show. "Even the cows know that."[98]

Victorians, preferring unchallenging mists and gentleness, would not know this for some time to come.

Yet Carr also knew that time is relative. Because art, like a baby in the womb, is not meant to gestate for longer than necessary. And what may seem to be years of fallow fields and unyielding crops may indeed be a time when an artist must work on other parts of her life and being. Sometimes, too, an event or an introduction to someone or a circle of friends, or simply a flash of inspiration while doing what Carr spent much of her time at—housework—is all it takes for an artist to realize her voice, her vision, her place on life's path. What it takes is a shift in what constitutes normalcy for that individual—something that breaks the roadblock. And that could just as well have been accepting the challenge of welcoming a monkey into her life. Woo's entrance into Carr's humdrum domestic reality clearly filled that purpose. And it served, as Kahlo's monkeys did, to protect her as she safely ventured into being who and what she really was—a fully formed artist with something new, something wonderful, to say.

"Fear," Carr wrote in a journal entry from July 1935, "is lack of faith."[99]

What was Emily Carr's fear—her lack of faith—based in? Mostly rejection, real or imagined. Richard Carr's favourite child, she had divorced herself from her father at age twelve in consequence of the "brutal telling." Her sisters criticized her lack of social graces, exiling her from the charmed circle of proper Victorian womanhood. Her mother, and her unconditional love, disappeared when Mrs. Carr died, "abandoning" her teenaged daughter. Her sisters did not believe that Emily had a future as artist. Victoria, where Carr spent most of her life, did not take notice of her art so much as it did her perceived eccentricities. Her duties as landlady made a charwoman of her. It would be completely understandable for a woman under these circumstances to simply sit down and say, "I cannot do more. This life is more than I can cope with. Where does art fit in?" Hence the generalized anxiety that had sent Carr to the

East Anglia Sanatorium in 1903 and continued to block her from moving forward in a productive way for years ahead.

By 1923, in the ten years since Hill House was built, Carr had been labouring daily as a harried landlady, janitor, mechanic and maid. What was meant to be an easy means of providing Carr an income on which to live and work as carefree artist became instead a burden of unremitting labour that ironically stripped away whatever time, energy and inspiration for art remained, according to Carr. The stress of her work as landlady, and Carr's volatile response to tenant problems on a daily basis, may have exacerbated the heart condition that was to incapacitate her for the last eight years of her life. Yet, as with most day jobs that go rogue despite one's best efforts, Carr's could have been worse. Whether her tenants were needy to an extraordinary degree; whether, as Carr believed, the disappearance of all the "good men" in the Great War filled the vacuum with unreliable human flotsam and jetsam; whether, as was demonstrably the case, the depression of rents and dearth of renters made Carr's life as landlady all the more miserable for being broke almost all the time while facing the demands of tenants for whom nothing seemed soon enough or good enough—Carr still managed to carry on. We also know she managed to continue to work on her art rather more than she herself indicated in her writings. In fact, Carr's problem as artist was not so much that tenants got in her way, any more than artists or writers who work jobs waiting tables or pushing papers around desks are entirely justified in blaming their need to make a living for their lack of making art. Years later, when she sold Hill House and left behind landladying for good, Carr quixotically professed to miss it, which is like saying she pined for all the stress, worry and interruption that had faced her on a daily basis. What she missed was the battle waged daily to find the time she thought she needed for her art—the opponent against which, with an irony Carr no doubt appreciated, she had to rage in order to dream more deeply, more courageously, into the thinking and making of art.

Fear had hounded Carr since childhood. Part of this was because she grew up in an era in which fear was a tool used to exact obedience from children and, specifically, from girls. With elder sisters who saw their role in life as models of Victorian self-control and selflessness—only one of her sisters (Clara, wife of Major John Nicholles of the Royal Engineers) ever married and left the family fold—Carr accompanied them to the stuffy garden parties of Victoria in a combined state of fear and dissent, knowing she would be required to do "the right thing" and unable to fulfill the contract demanded of the daughter of a well-to-do paterfamilias, knowing she also had the exhilarating opportunity to show a conventional world just what unconventionality she was capable of by spilling tea or mussing her dress. Any pleasure Carr may have derived from upsetting the settled status quo was offset by sharp criticisms from her sisters for her lack of social graces and a lifelong difficulty controlling impulses that made her father state he thought she should have been born a boy rather than a girl (a telling commentary on freedom relative to males and females of the Victorian period). She needed to assert her individuality, regardless of how it was received; she wanted to assert herself as artist, regardless of her sisters' opinions ("They always made me feel as if my painting was indecent"[100]) and the public's response—and did so at the cost of many sleepless nights. By any standard, under these circumstances it has to be said that her survival as artist is arguably her greatest achievement.

But perhaps the missing ingredient, as Carr herself understood, was not just faith instead of fear, but love.

Carr seemed to accept that whatever happened to her, however painful, occurred for what must be an edifying reason, a teaching moment that had to sting, like the harsh medicines of her childhood, to be effective. "This being alone," she wrote, "must be to teach me something." So, too, she suggested in her journals, must be her lifelong effort to maintain a belief in love itself, despite the fact love often seemed one-sided. She could not keep the need to nurture this belief out of her life, however much she wished it had never grown there, "wasted and unwanted." Even when she pulled it out, she wrote, roots and all, the flower would not die, even when she threw it on stones. Indeed, Carr realized that only when "the dust [that] is the love of the blessed creatures, monkey and dogs and blessed little rat offering the rootlets of my love nourishment and shelter" did she understand the durability, the imperative, of love in her life.[101]

Woo's appearance in Carr's life seemed to mark a turning point for her as artist, and that turning point seems to have been made possible by a confrontation with those fears that had kept Carr in a developmental limbo. Few who knew Carr, even those who saw her adoring her dogs, rat, cat and birds, would disagree that Woo was the very apex of that love. It was a love that seriously changed Carr's life in ways difficult to unpack, like a planet too distant to be seen, but whose gravitational pull on satellites around it proved that it was there, undeniable.

We know about Lawren Harris and Mark Tobey and their influence on Carr. We recognize that Carr learned a great deal from the reality-bending and reality-enhancing distortions and the complex natural symbolism of Indigenous carving and painting. But the heart can't help but go to other places the mind cannot verify. So let's take it there. Let's imagine Woo alone one day in Carr's Simcoe Street studio.

She has been left momentarily while Carr, just as she prepares to start a painting, hurries off to fetch something or to deal with an irate tenant or to tend to a dog crying in the garden kennels. In true Woo fashion, the monkey unhooks her chain and bolts for the blank new canvas Carr has stretched and left sitting at an angle on its easel.

Dr. Shigeru Watanabe, professor of psychology at Keio University in Japan, who has researched animals' responses to art, pointed out that in order to appreciate art, two qualities are needed: there must be the ability to perceive and discern, and the faculty of sensory response to what one perceives—notably, pleasure. These are factors assumed to exist in the mental and emotional equipment of art-loving and art-creating human beings. Based on his research, Dr. Watanabe suggests these factors are known to animals too. How much more so, then, might this be true of a monkey who spent most of her time in an artist's studio, in an artist's life? Through watching Carr at work, Woo may not have understood what she was doing (on par with many artists, who often wonder the same thing about their own actions), but she had developed an appreciation for her activity as something that mattered to Carr, the sort of seeking activity that to Woo might have been analogous to scanning the shallows for crabs or Ginger Pop's coat for tasty flakes of dandruff. Two very different animals may yet still understand what brings pleasure to another, and be curious about, seek and experience the source that brings it.[102]

The white rectangle gathers light from the windows; nearby, a palette glistens with those pigments whose colours Woo may not be able to distinguish as Carr does, but the significance of which has been deeply impressed on her, for they take a great deal of the attention Woo herself constantly seeks. Woo glances about warily, then takes Carr's brush in a delicate brown hand, the bristles wet with colour, and does as she has seen Carr do. She splats the brush on the blank challenge of the canvas's surface. It slides, colour streams forth, and the monkey understands. Perhaps the brush is loaded with blue, or green, or yellow. It does not matter. Woo lets the brush, and perhaps also her sharp black nails, slip over the surface in a billow of hue, as if the heavens were no more than an azure bed sheet filled with the four winds, rattling and snapping like laundry in a breeze, trees rippling against the sky like their reflections in water, a sun shedding waterfalls of brightness. "It's scientifically demonstrable," says Dr. Richard Prum, evolutionary ornithologist at Yale, "that animals have an aesthetic capacity." They have the capacity to perceive and evaluate, he adds, and the motivation to act upon those factors whether in repulsion or attraction. "That in and of itself makes for an aesthetic experience," he says.[103]

She guides the brush again, rhythmically, as she has seen the ocean move, its rows and layers of blue shouldering their way forward to flat and final oneness with the shore. Woo does not do what she does because she is an artist. Woo does what she does with Carr's brush because Woo is just Woo. What, after all, is art? Emily Carr might step out to her garden on a starry night and there above her lie all the ornaments of astronomy—the Big Dipper, Orion's Belt, the Seven Sisters, forms she could name. Yet from some other vantage point as distant as another galaxy, or as close as a different world seen through the golden eyes of Woo, what were these shapes when viewed from some other part of the stage of lived experience, where Woo happened to view them? What new forms unveiled against the night? But that is the secret of art, isn't it, to see with different eyes, and to have the courage and conviction to present that new vision to the world? In Woo's world, there are no similes, no efforts to capture something remembered. What she sees, *is*.

The experiment ends abruptly when the doorway is filled with the returning figure of Carr, exasperated, or singing to herself. Into the studio, finished with her task, Carr rushes and then stops. Woo drops the brush messily into the smeared palette and departs to her corner, refastening the chain; she sits and looks at Carr. Carr is amused and says something funny to Woo, who blinks up at her. Then Carr looks at the canvas and something more than just a sky opens before her. Carr gazes at Woo's splash of sky, and wonders, with her, what new thing unfurls itself there, a reality she has sought and never found—till now.

Woo's doodles, forgotten as she sits chewing her chain, what might they stand for in the long, hard-fought, hard-won battle of Carr's growth as artist, her struggle to breach the surface of acceptability, to gulp the bracing air of daring, the challenge of why not?

It was Pablo Picasso who confessed that it took him only a few years to learn how to paint like the Renaissance artist and architect Raphael, but an entire lifetime to paint with the simplicity, the directness, the unforced whimsy of a child. It was this bracing wave of freedom that Carr expressed through all her work from the late 1920s onward. Couldn't Woo have found that freedom too? Found it first? It's not impossible. Referring to animal creativity, Dr. Jane Goodall noted she was willing to accord animals the possibility, the belief, that they, like humans, were able to appreciate and participate in creative endeavours in various forms.[104]

Surely Emily Carr, who did not live as many humans seemed to do, with an impermeable wall between themselves and animals, came to something like the same conclusion. "There is no 'we' in animal life," Carr wrote in 1935, giving them the ultimate benefit. "It is 'I.'"[105] She could have said the same of the life of an artist. Art was about working together with the singleness of purpose of an individual force—with past and present, heart and mind, and with whatever muse one needed to help one cross the connecting bridge, even a muse like Woo.

CHAPTER 5

"Artists Are Lovers"

There is a wealth of local lore in Victoria about how Carr, with her dogs and Woo, pushed a baby carriage as a makeshift shopping trolley on expeditions downtown, leading her menagerie audaciously past curtain-twitching dowagers and sidewalk pedestrian double-takes.

Is there an image of Emily Carr more indelibly etched on Canadian cultural memory than this? I venture to suggest this image is as powerful in its way as any of Carr's paintings, and for the same reason—what it tells us about the artist. What sets the image off as unique, rather than simply unusual, is the presence of Woo. Because where a lady walking many small dogs is apt to pass without much more notice than the visual charm warrants, a monkey adds a wild card. And where Carr is concerned, it's a mesmerizing combination, one that has been seized on by illustrators, who often show us some version of Woo, walking about in a brightly coloured skirt, Carr in dowdy hat or headband and shapeless smock as she leads Woo and a parade of yapping little dogs and animals of assorted other species.

My question has always been, when she made her animals public in this manner, what did Carr think she was doing? What did she want to do?

Anyone who has read Astrid Lindgren's Pippi Longstocking books, the first of which was published the year of Carr's death, will notice a similarity between the title character and Carr: an unconventional girl with a distant, idolized father who lives on her own, respects no rules, loves animals, has a monkey (Mr. Nilsson) and doesn't care what people think. These are qualities notable for a child; society expected and preferred children to be under the aegis of some authority, whether parent or some other controlling entity. Pippi flouted this rule, and to a degree got away with it precisely because she was a child. Carr, whose behaviour may well have been seen as childish for a middle-aged woman, could not hide behind a little girl's naïveté. But as she pushed her pram about town, it could be said she couldn't have cared any less about the opinion of her fellow Victorians than she did most conventional expectations. She used the pram not just for her dogs but for far more workaday purposes, such as bringing back joints of meat and bones from the butcher's, or when she needed it to transport clay she had dug from the cliffs at Dallas Road, from which she shaped and painted the objects—vases, lamp bases, cigarette dishes—baked in her make-shift kiln for sale to the tourist trade. Surely that, too, along with all the animals, drew more stares and fuelled more rumours as to her eccentricity. We know Carr was not that simple to diagnose. Carr's friend Edythe Hembroff-Schleicher believed these walks were for "a solid practical reason," noting that Woo was never carried but made to walk, as part of the exercise Carr required of her dogs, and cast doubt on this "classic example of her eccentricity" as having occurred more than a few times—though those few times were clearly enough to capture and set her reputation in stone among Victoria locals.[106] Yet it's a fair question. What indeed was Carr doing when she paraded with her animals in this manner? Was it perhaps an act not so much of public audacity as of public honesty? As Dr. Phyllis Marie Jensen suggests, "In fact, her monkey is an example of her openness."[107]

Carol Pearson suggested long ago that this was the case. She recalled an occasion when she went walking downtown with Carr to go shopping. With Woo attached to the pram handle by her chain, and one or more of the dogs in the carriage or following it en route to market, Pearson wrote, Carr was targeted by a "crowd" from which issued "all sorts of remarks, mostly unkind, some rude."[108] Pearson understood that Carr, as Jensen suggests, was no shrinking violet stunned by adverse public reception to her perceived eccentricities. Carr clearly expected and was prepared for reaction—as may be, perhaps desired it—but above all, she did not care. When Pearson consoled Carr after one of these insulting experiences on the streets of town, Carr laughed. "It is they who should be pitied," she assured Pearson. "They may have no real interest in life, no pets of their own."[109] This is but partly bravado. It is also partly theatre. It is mostly compassion.

New York artist Allen Hirsch is renowned for his portraiture, of himself and others, and his brilliant use of a variety of media to tell stories about people and the worlds they live in. For fourteen years, Hirsch lived with a capuchin monkey whom he called Benjamin. Hirsch had rescued the orphaned infant in Venezuela, brought him back to New York City and found that through Benjamin, whom he carried on his shoulder through the streets of Manhattan, his life was changed, as artist and as man. As Hirsch told me in a recent interview, "I was a strange kid in school and followed my own beat, which usually attracted attention—by design or not. When I walked Benjamin around Soho, we certainly drew attention but I felt more the pride of a parent. This animated leprechaun of a creature lit up the faces of anyone who saw him. He represented something that was lost in that humanity; I felt I was bringing a living work of art into that oppressive city." Hirsch said, "I brought out the human in him and he brought out the monkey in me." It seemed clear to me: for both Carr and Hirsch (both having been kids who did not fit in, both grownups who wisely learned not to bother trying), sharing their monkey with a public that might accept or reject, be delighted or unmoved by that sharing, was part and parcel of the same process involved in a public art show. "Here is my great work of love," Carr might have said to the good people of Victoria. "Artists are lovers," noted Hirsch. "And Benjamin was a vehicle for me to love infinitely, without boundaries. While I was with him, I was continually aware of this blessing and felt gratitude to be able to love like that. Expressing love is the highest motivating force behind art. While this means pouring feelings through paint on a surface, Benjamin," said Hirsch, "was a living vessel of my love." It's not hard to see that Carr might well agree. Animals, it is quite clear, were the only vessels who could handle the volume of Emily Carr's love. As with Allen Hirsch and Benjamin, they brought out the best in each other.[110]

And Woo served as catalyst for interactions between Carr and other people that served to change them as much as bringing about change in Carr herself. On one memorable occasion Carr wrote about in *The Heart of the Peacock,* she and Woo were in Beacon Hill Park when they met two gentlemen, "dignified professors," the last people one would expect to be so enchanted with Woo they would without further ado get "down on their hands and knees, stalking grasshoppers to please the appetite of a diminutive scarlet-aproned monkey."[111] Woo seems to have enabled those who encountered her to see the world in a way different from before, to forget one was a respectable person wearing suit and tie, and descend to the level of Mother Earth, where all animals and Carr herself felt most at home, where there was truth in the embrace of dirt, grass, leaves. But we must at least suggest that in some part, as with Allen Hirsch and Benjamin, public appearance together also became public performance and public art too. As Hirsch said about Benjamin, carrying him around Soho on his shoulder "was like bringing a Broadway show to every street corner,"[112] and such would appear to be the case with Woo and Carr, whether their audiences were mothers with their hair in curlers, pausing in their routine walks so their children could admire the monkey in Carr's window, or academics kneeling in pinstripes in a public park to find tasty insect morsels for Woo to feast on. Woo normalized in the everyday world that sense of spectacle one usually enjoyed at Christmas or Halloween, if one were an adult who had not lost touch with one's childhood—at all times, if one were still blessed to be a child.

Carr wrote of her garden that "it was just ordinary—common flowers, everyday shrubs, apple-trees ... its southern limit was the straight square shadow of my apartment house"—but we know she considered it such a special place that it was designed for her use alone. Thus an invitation to share it for tea was an honour, as no doubt many of those she asked to a tea party there would have appreciated. As the tea party was not long after Woo came to Hill House, the occasion was even more special because it was the first time Carr's friends would get to meet Woo.[113]

Woo seemed keen enough on the whole thing, because once outside she immediately climbed up to her box in the cherry tree, where she crouched looking down at the guests as they arrived by the side gate. With each arrival, however, the monkey's excitement and anxiety grew.

Carr wrote that her guests greeted her first, then, spotting the monkey, whom they saw as "joint hostess" of the tea party, headed toward her cherry tree "as people entering a room go straight to an open fire." Woo "stood upright and gave a throaty croak," whether greeting or warning was unclear, for more people had gathered and were staring up at her, heads thrown back to catch what glimpses they could of the hairy little figure in a dress sitting above. Woo's human qualities seemed to fascinate them, "the neatness and precision of those strong slender little fingers." As the guests watched, Carr coaxed Woo down from the tree and played This Little Piggy with the monkey. Woo held up each hand and then each foot, observing with interest as Carr told each "piggy." After Carr had sent all the pigs home, Woo carefully examined each hand, front and back, and then again, as if some sort of magic rite had been spoken over them, as if they must be special if the human mother who was the centre of her world had taken the trouble to do so, but that as they were her fingers and toes, it was difficult to see them as anything but utilitarian.[114]

Woo climbed back up to her box, and then a pair of women guests arrived in the garden. They stood staring up at Woo with something like the voyeuristic hauteur of visitors to a zoo, and Carr overheard them remarking on the human-like qualities of Woo's hands, while at the same time casting aspersion on Charles Darwin for being so ridiculous as to conclude that humans and simians could possibly be descendants of the same ancestor. How could the creature have hands like ours, albeit quite hairy, and yet no brain to speak of? One of the women said, "The humanness of her makes me sick!"[115]

Evidently these guests had not read Darwin's *The Expression of the Emotions in Man and Animals*. "The various species and genera of monkeys express their feelings in many different ways," wrote Darwin, "and this fact is interesting, as in some degree bearing on the question, whether the so-called races of man should be ranked as distinct species or varieties; for ... the different races of man express their emotions and sensations with remarkable uniformity throughout the world. Some of the expressive actions of monkeys are interesting in another way, namely from being closely analogous to those of man."[116]

Carr may not have read Darwin's book either, but she had long ago come to the same conclusion where animals were concerned. Stepping up to the women, she commented briskly, "She has sense enough to be her own amusing self," referring to Woo. "Few of us have that." Woo was a "small, intelligent beast," Carr added, not a "tenth-rate human being."[117]

Trying to tease the increasingly reticent Woo out of her box, another couple of guests began amusing themselves by prodding Woo with sticks. The monkey bared her teeth, grabbed the sticks and broke them. "Savage little beast!" the guests said, laughing.[118] We can wonder why Carr, witnessing this, held her cool. Were the offenders colleagues she couldn't afford to alienate? Did she not wish to add more fuel to the urban legend of the crazy monkey lady of Victoria? Or did she have a special trick up her sleeve?

Leaving the garden for a moment, Carr went upstairs and brought back down one of Woo's little hand mirrors. She lifted it up to Woo, still crouching angrily in her box. There was an instantaneous change. Woo took up the mirror, turned her back on Carr's guests and stared adoringly at her reflection for the duration of the tea party. Carr wrote, "I was more furious than Woo. All she asked was to be let alone," to pursue in peace "her own investigations of humans." It was the "shadow of her own kind," ultimately, that proved of more interest than the humans below, relegated to their teacups and plates of scones, the inference being that that simian shadow's company was far superior to theirs.[119]

Over forty years later, psychologist Gordon G. Gallup would test a variety of primates to determine whether they were able to recognize themselves in a reflective surface. He placed some of them in front of mirrors for hours at a time, introducing others to mirrors with a dab of red on the forehead. His published study reported that chimpanzees were quickest to recognize their own reflections, orangutans next down the list and gorillas at the bottom, and among the chimps there were some who did not react to the mirror at all. But for the most part, they were the first to do so. Macaques like Woo, however, did worse than the gorillas, according to Gallup. Psychologist Merlin Donald pointed out that not one of the monkey species tested by Gallup was able to pass the mirror test—to appear to be aware, when looking in a mirror, that they were seeing a reflection of themselves.[120] In more recent years, tests have been conducted at the Shanghai Institutes for Biological Sciences by neuroscientist Neng Gong, in which macaques were trained (using restraint and negative reinforcement) to touch a place on their faces to which, in front of a mirror, a laser beam was directed, the successful monkey being given a treat as reward. Gallup doubts this is true recognition; given the coercion involved, it may not be.[121] Peter Wohlleben, in his powerful, intimate look into animals' inner lives, noted that the mirror test has been applied to dolphins, elephants and pigs, with apparent success, adding that it is important to remember that only we know the mirror as a mirror.[122] In *her* mirror image, Woo saw, as Carr rightly noted, who she was. She didn't need science to tell her this, but as legal scholar Steven W. Wise, leading proponent of legally recognized personhood for animals, succinctly reminds us, "Remember, because no one can ever know for certain that anyone, human or nonhuman, has a mind, all we can do is apply our reasoned judgment to the facts that science reveals."[123]

Does scientific opinion mean all monkeys have no sense of self, no recognition of identity? If that is true, what was Woo doing as she looked in her mirror? Or perhaps the better question is: What was Carr telling her friends when she handed the mirror to her monkey? Was she saying that, regardless of those who disparaged Darwin for including monkeys in the human family tree, and regardless of scientists, lab experiments and strict deliverables based on ticked boxes, Woo did indeed have a sense of self, that she knew who she was? That as a self-aware being, she deserved better than to be stared at and teased? And perhaps Carr was also telling Woo, "To thine own self be true—and ignore the great apes making fools of themselves on the lawn below!"[124]

Woo would have other encounters with her great ape cousins that would compete with the rudeness and cluelessness of the people at that garden party, incapable of according her the basic respect she deserved as a living being, oblivious to lessons she might have to teach them about dignity and integrity of self. This is where Carr tells us the other side to this story, about the time Woo helped teach a human humanity, without even trying.

Some time after 1923, while Woo was still getting her bearings, an elderly, well-to-do and highly proper lady had come to Hill House to meet Carr about renting a suite. Carr calls her Mrs. Pinker, a name that sounds rich with Dickensian satire, in that a less pink lady is difficult to imagine. Mrs. Pinker sounds particularly grey, one of those Victorian widows who indulged in nothing more decorative than the sombre gleam of jet brooches, black fox furs from which the bloom had gone and a lorgnette that dangled when it was not being lifted to inspect menus, the post and the society column. Underscoring this sober broadcloth impression, Mrs. Pinker was a friend of Lizzie's and so was possibly part of her prayer circle. Lizzie tried to warn her sister prior to the elderly Mrs. Pinker's arrival: "She hates monkeys." Carr's reply: too bad. "Love me, love my monk," she said. Lizzie probably briefed Mrs. Pinker on the situation she would find at Hill House because, according to Carr, the first words out of her mouth on stepping over the threshold were, “I don’t like monkeys.” She went on to cite past experience with them at a hotel in Madeira, Portugal, where the pet primates of aristocratic ladies apparently ran berserk through the lobby, affronting decent society, or so her recollection had it.[125]

It was not that Mrs. Pinker disliked animals in general. When she entered Carr’s studio and found that dogs and the cat were occupying all soft surfaces, she chose to sit on a cushionless wooden chair and professed herself shocked when Carr ordered the animals to scatter and make a more comfortable place for her guest—a sign that gave Carr hope. However, it was puzzling that Mrs. Pinker was fixated most of all on Woo, who was not even in the room. Where was she? Mrs. Pinker asked Carr, who informed her she was in the basement with Ginger Pop, so as not to make a fuss. Mrs. Pinker was adamant—she must meet this monkey, even if she already knew she hated her. So Carr dutifully went downstairs, and soon up ahead of her heavy tread came the excited clicking of Ginger Pop’s claws. Then the silent but potent vibrancy of a monkey entered the studio behind him—Woo, wearing her dress and with her chain in her mouth.

When she saw Mrs. Pinker, wrote Carr, Woo “made a face and let out a squeal,” unwittingly affirming the lady’s negative opinion of monkeys in all pertinent details. Woo then took that antagonism a step further. Something about her attracted Mrs. Pinker, who made a gesture of polite friendliness toward the monkey. Woo’s response was to suddenly steal up to Mrs. Pinker’s chair and yank a ball of yarn from her lap. Carr ordered Woo to return the wool to where she had found it. Instead, Woo threw it at Mrs. Pinker’s feet. Then, when Mrs. Pinker reached down for the wool, Woo extended one of her slender arms, its silvery fur clashing with the sleeve of her floral calico and canvas pinafore, and sharply slapped the old lady with the flat of her hand.[126]

This should have helped Mrs. Pinker make up her mind about whether to take up residence in Hill House. Yet again, something about Woo—Carr, a witness, does not speculate what—made Mrs. Pinker stay seated. A psychologist might say Mrs. Pinker was anthropomorphizing Woo, that seeing her at close range, as opposed to her distant view of the anarchic primates in the Portuguese hotel, made Woo seem more child than beast—a child who should know better than to perpetrate these naughty acts on respectable people but had certain redeeming charms nonetheless. Who in her day, when young people were to be seen and not heard, did not hold to this belief where children were concerned? And as is well known, unbridged distance from an object or being causing fear or unease is one of the prime ingredients for prejudice. Monkeys scaling a marble staircase in a hotel and a monkey sitting at one's feet with one's ball of yarn were not simply two different settings; it may have appeared to Mrs. Pinker that she was dealing with two different concepts of monkey.

Whatever the case, the old lady kept her seat and as she knitted, she keenly watched Carr's menagerie, focusing especially on Woo. After remonstrating with her, Carr secured the monkey's chain. Mrs. Pinker forgotten, Woo pulled Ginger Pop over to her by an ear, and soon both were engaged in play. Carr noticed Mrs. Pinker's smile, then was startled by her outright laughter when Woo, seizing on her human "mother's" inattention, stole her handkerchief and used it to wash Ginger Pop's face, a gesture she had learned through visits to Alice's school at bath time. Clearly, Carr need not have worried about Mrs. Pinker. Through her laughter, she made it clear she was at Hill House to stay, not despite the monkey but because of her.

After that, Mrs. Pinker asked to see Woo every day, and was soon knitting a garment for her in a vivid red wool. Woo wore the jumper dutifully on an excursion with Carr and the dogs to Beacon Hill Park, only to rip it off and toss it in a treetop. Woo, Carr thought, clearly knew she looked like a mad poinsettia dashing around the green space, and was better off being less conspicuous. It's just as likely Woo did this because she was still wary of Mrs. Pinker, and the jumper smelled of her, and perhaps also because the garment was so different from the frocks Carr had trained her to wear. Happily, Mrs. Pinker never knew what happened to the jumper. In fact, it seemed nothing Woo did could depreciate her affection for the monkey. Even when Mrs. Pinker lay ill in bed, and on one occasion was deprived of the ministrations of a visiting doctor because he caught sight of Woo and ended up playing with her on the floor, underneath the old lady's impatience was real admiration for—and perhaps even an envy of—the spirit of a creature who knew no restraint except her chain and the occasional admonition from Carr, the one human she obeyed (when she felt like it).

There was another facet to this dynamic that both Mrs. Pinker and Carr may have shared through the vector of the irrepressible energy and honesty of Woo. Both prickly in personality, long practised in keeping other people at a safe distance, neither particularly gifted in overcoming those traits, the elderly lady and the landlady-artist may have seen in Woo an unhindered display of a joy in life they wished they could share. For Woo had a knack for celebrating honest responses to all situations among humans, even those who professed to despise and fear her. If there is one thing of which we can be sure about the otherwise mysterious Woo, because it is the one thing we can be sure about any animal, it's that everything she did came from a place of truth, of honest motivation and guileless act. After all, as philosopher John Gray admonished his fellow *Homo sapiens*, we would do well to seek ethics not just among humankind but among those members of our extended biological family—animals.[127]

CHAPTER 6

"One Is So Obviously Their God"

From public life to private life, Carr's animals—especially Woo—were so much a part of the fabric of everything the artist did, from daily routines to sketching trips to Beacon Hill Park and camping trips farther afield, that they seemed to her friend Edythe Hembroff-Schleicher as if they were constantly underfoot, no matter where Carr happened to be. During their stay at a cramped remote cottage, from which the women hiked to the wilderness with their paintboxes and easels, Edythe wrote with annoyance of "the temper-trying huddle of beasts, possessions, artists. We stepped over dogs and on dogs." She's careful to point out that *she* was the one annoyed by the animals—it was Carr who was annoyed by too close proximity to *her*.[128]

If, like her nineteenth-century Yorkshire sister in spirit, Emily Brontë, Carr would "walk where my own nature would be leading,"[129] she, like Brontë, was also unable to truly follow her own nature without her animal family at her side (another similarity to Brontë, with her devoted dog, Keeper). "Her abiding love for all animals flowed deep," wrote Dr. Phyllis Marie Jensen.[130] Her creatures, as Carr called them, using the word in its most endearing sense, had to always be with her, however impractical. And they seemed to understand that for these outings, they were on a special mission, one requiring best behaviour. Carr's friend Carol Pearson wrote that as she and Carr sketched, "the animals seemed to know they were to have their fun quietly, and they did."[131] The amazing thing to many outsiders who met Carr's menagerie was that though some of them were by nature predators of others, and there were animosities (as between Dolf the cat and Woo) that always simmered under the surface, yet they coexisted in peaceful acceptance of one another. One of Carr's friends, the violinist and composer Murray Adaskin, recalled visiting Carr when she was camping with her animals. Though they were cheek by jowl in their sleeping boxes in a small space, the dogs, cat, rat, birds and monkey got along in perfect serenity, in much the way well-bred, considerate humans were capable of treating one another.[132] Pearson was to witness a singular example of Woo's altruism in this regard. For a camping trip with Carr, all the animals had been secured as usual in their travelling boxes, the doors tied with twine, and though the animals were stressed by a taxi ride to their embarkation point, they then had to wait as the friend who was supposed to meet Carr was delayed. Woo began to fidget so much that Carr released her from her cage. Pearson noted that the first thing the monkey did was to go from one animal's box to another, trying to undo the knots in the twine and let them out.[133]

Woo actually saved the life of one of her animal housemates. According to Carr, Woo, with her preference for griffons, was not especially attached to the cat Dolf, whom Carr described as her "enemy." When Dolf went missing for four days, Carr feared that he had been hit by a car—he was, she said, the colour of dusk, and was often to be seen crossing Simcoe Street in the dark. Carr took Woo on her chain and roamed the neighbourhood to see if she could find the cat. Carr at first suspected Dolf had got into a house next door that no one lived in, and was trying to see through one of its dusty windows when Woo insisted on pulling her away. Clambering over the garden grass, Woo stopped near a flowering shrub, reached in a hand and pulled something out to show Carr. It was a bunch of Dolf's grey fur. Carr looked under the shrub and found an injured Dolf lying on the ground, bleeding. It was clear he had been struck by an automobile in the street. He had seemingly dragged himself as close to Hill House as he could. Carr got the cat to Hill House and though his wounds were severe, she nursed him back to health, pointing out that had he not been located when he was, he would likely have died. "He made complete recovery," Carr wrote, "and lived for eight years after that, dying at the fine old age of eighteen years." She noted that even then Woo and Dolf would have nothing to do with each other. But then, that is the truest form of altruism, isn't it—to save your enemy as you would save your friend?[134]

Still, if Woo got along with most of Carr's animal family, if only by acknowledging them as members of the same household, she could be decidedly hostile toward her own species, a reaction more likely due to a complex series of circumstances in a history about which nobody could know, but that Carr concluded was due to the bullying suffered at the hands of the other monkeys in Lucy Cowie's shop—a sense of being the odd man out being something Carr, growing up, felt she and the monkey had in common.

Lucy Cowie re-entered Woo's life because she had a favour to ask of Carr. The pet store owner had to leave Victoria for a short time. While she had someone to mind her store, there was nobody to look after her own monkey, Mitsey. Cowie told Carr that her assistant at the Bird and Pet Shop was not comfortable with Mitsey (a strange aversion considering where the assistant worked), and Cowie wondered whether Carr would take Mitsey for the week she would be away. Carr doesn't tell us what kind of monkey Mitsey was, but it is safe to assume that she was also a macaque, Lucy Cowie's preferred import. Carr was enthusiastic about having Mitsey at Hill House, thinking that Woo would rejoice to see one of her own kind. When Cowie walked into Carr's studio, Mitsey in her arms, she found Woo sitting on the hearth bench, scowling "furiously," as if she had divined by some higher sense that a rival was being introduced into the household. Her mood got worse as Carr attempted to make Mitsey feel at home. Cowie placed Mitsey on one end of the bench from Woo, as if expecting the two to instantly be arm in arm. That was not the case. Woo had Ginger Pop with her, and kept him at arm's length, as far from Mitsey as she could reach, baring her teeth.[135] One reads of this encounter with the same unease as when contemplating the cavalier way Carr had introduced Woo to the dogs. Had Carr been a parent, it's easy to envision her tossing her child into the deep end of a swimming pool as the best way to teach it how to swim. There was a similar danger in what was happening in the studio between Woo and Mitsey. Had Woo been sufficiently provoked, she might have attacked, injured or even killed the more reticent Mitsey. It goes without saying that Ginger Pop, sitting at close quarters with Woo, could have been hurt in the process.

But Carr believed in letting nature take its course (unless she could justify interference, as she so often did). While the teeth-baring and shrieking took place, she stood back and watched with Cowie, who was possibly wondering whether to leave Mitsey here after all, as Ginger Pop slowly pulled away from Woo's grasp, his little nose working busily toward Mitsey's unfamiliar scent. Noting this, Woo suddenly jumped across from the bench and, like a jealous wife, slapped Ginger Pop, pulling him back to her by one of his ears. Then, according to Carr, the crisis suddenly passed. In fact, Carr suggests that Ginger Pop's friendliness toward Mitsey moved Woo to consider showing Mitsey more cordiality. Still grasping Ginger Pop's ear, Woo cautiously scooted toward the other monkey who, whether from courage or terror, remained frozen to the edge of the bench. Finally, Woo not only unbent enough to sit beside Mitsey, but put an arm around her (though still gripping Ginger Pop protectively with the other hand). On Lucy Cowie's departure, the monkeys seemed to be fast friends.[136]

Carr got Mitsey into a dress (perhaps one of Woo's spares) and took the monkeys out to her back garden. There, in the comparative freedom of grass, trees and sky, where they could gambol and dig as they wished, Woo and Mitsey now played as if they had always known each other. Carr decided it was safe to go further and took the monkeys down to the beach. Mitsey joined Woo in searching the water for crabs, as their cousins in Java did. Carr rejoiced that she had finally found a friend for Woo who was of her own species. But when the week was over and it came time for Lucy Cowie to fetch Mitsey away, there was no scene of repining, at least on Woo's part. If Mitsey left Hill House looking back at Woo from Mrs. Cowie's arms, it was an interest that was decidedly not returned, as Carr tells us. It was also clear that Woo's brief friendship with Mitsey was indeed a one-off. When a friend came to Hill House with two of her pet monkeys, they and Woo were soon miserable together, alternately sulking and erupting in shrieks in Carr's garden. "My own belief," wrote Carr, "is that Woo preferred the companionship and admiration of human beings."[137] How had Woo arrived in Victoria unsocialized to her own kind? Had she already been someone's pet before being brought to North America and sold? Even today, primates are found throughout Asia tied to a wall or post, never close enough to their captors to form a relationship across the species barrier, and if raised away from fellow monkeys or apes, they grow up unable to understand the complex language of sounds, expressions and gestures habitual to their own species. These solitary animals, like dogs kept in locked cages in the canine prison camps known as puppy mills, develop additional complexes on top of being deprived of the contact necessary for all levels of communication. Placing such animals in proximity to those who have been normally socialized can create fear in one, bafflement in the other, and does nothing to bridge a gap that may never be crossed. So far as we know, Woo chose only two dogs—Ginger Pop and another griffon, Koko—and one human, Carr, as her significant others. This discomfort with other monkeys, except for the brief time with Mitsey, and why Mitsey was tolerated while others were not, is just one among the many mysteries of Woo's background and, especially, just one of the many mysteries of Woo.

Another of these mysteries was one that has always fascinated and troubled me, but one I suspect has a lot to do with the monkey's attachment to Carr—Woo's repeated ingesting of Carr's paints, in toxic quantities that nearly killed her. In childhood, we are all told by our mothers not to eat this or that, and some of us decide to see what this inedible substance is all about anyway, and pay the painful consequences with an emergency room stomach pump. That experience is usually sufficient to keep us from trying to eat that forbidden substance ever again. The same holds true for many animals, and as such one would expect it to hold especially true for an intelligent monkey like Woo. She endured the consequences more than once, though surely knowing what the results would be. So my question has always been not why she kept doing it, but were the results she endured, however upsetting, precisely the ones she desired?

In 2002, Sir David Attenborough hosted a BBC series, *Life of Mammals*. In one of the segments, Attenborough visits Camp Leakey, a sanctuary in Borneo for orangutans rescued from captivity and returned to forests of which many of them must have had—like Woo—only remote recollection. We see a mother orang paddling a canoe to shore, where she sits on a dock and washes socks, scrubbing them with soap and rinsing them in the water, then washing her hands. She later takes a saw and, under the admiring gaze of Attenborough, begins working on a piece of wood, into which she hammers nails, all while her baby sits under her arm, bright-eyed and taking in every detail. Attenborough points out that the viewer's first impression might be that this orangutan had been taught these things, after the fashion of animals trained to do tricks in a circus. Not true. She was performing these tasks solely on her own initiative. She had seen others doing these tasks, Attenborough explains, and what we see as imitation is actually very similar to our human learning process—learning from what we observe in others, and using tools to carry out those tasks, arguably the two most significant abilities humans have used to change their world.[138]

Memory is something we take for granted in humans, forget to consider in our animal cousins and consign to mere mimicry in primates. There are few more heartbreaking examples of this than when British businessman and conservationist Damian Aspinall, who had raised a male gorilla, Kwibi, in England till age five, then returned him to the wild, was greeted by Kwibi after a separation of five more years as if no time had passed, and then deeply mourned when he left;[139] or when Dr. Jane Goodall, in June 2013, helped release a chimpanzee called Wounda onto Tchindzoulou Island, a sanctuary in Congo, and after being let out of her cage, Wounda turned not to race happily into the jungle but to Goodall, enfolding her in an embrace.[140]

Woo imitated many of the activities she saw Carr doing. But besides the replicating of tasks and use of tools, these efforts to do what Carr did bear out another level of awareness—a keen memory of feelings, an attribute humans are not particularly generous in granting to our primate cousins, and the acting out on those feelings in physical demonstrations of affection. Carol Pearson remembered how, during packing for a camping trip with Carr, she found that Woo had managed to fill a suitcase with "discarded fruit, insoles from shoes" and everything and anything else she seemed to think necessary for the trip, including house keys she had made off with right under Carr's nose.[141]

When we say a person is copying another almost exactly, not quite but to a degree believed to be indicative of the copier having no original ideas of his own, we say he is "aping" that other person, "ape" referring to a primate's alleged unoriginal obsession with copying what it sees others doing—"monkey see, monkey do." As with so many human failings we describe in terms referencing animals, the latter are actually usually doing what they do for reasons far more complex and layered than we give them credit for. Woo didn't simply copy what she observed. She clearly wanted to do the same things her human mother did, much as she would have done beside her biological mother—hunting, social interaction with the females of their matriarchy and other life skills—in the jungle lagoons of Java. Acts of washing hands or clothes, of sewing, cooking (not actually doing any of these but going precisely through the motions as she understood them), were occasions for Woo to show Carr that she was paying attention, that what Carr did mattered to her enough to do them also, and perhaps doing what Carr did was also a way of showing dependence and trust. Woo, watching Carr, was trying her hand at doing all the things Carr did, after the pattern established from her first day in the house. And in packing her own "things" in the suitcase, Woo may have been telling Carr how much she wanted to be with her and not to be left behind. Perhaps, also, there was some jealousy toward Pearson, who might be trying to take Carr away from her. It is quite possible such jealousy was in play when, as Edythe Hembroff-Schleicher remembered, during a camping trip together, along with all the animals, packed into a tiny cabin, Woo urinated in one of Carr's shoes (and, shockingly, was given "the spanking of her life" by Carr in consequence).[142]

Woo's possessiveness of Carr was displayed for all to see during a visit to the artist's studio by a group of people interested in her paintings. When Carr's guests were occupied with pictures, they were also occupied with Carr, and Woo, chained in her corner, could not see Carr or get to her. Pearson relates watching as Woo unhooked her chain and scurried to where there was a stack of magazines. She carefully peeled one off the pile and took it back to her corner, as if wanting to read in peace and quiet. She opened it to look at the pages, remaining well within sight of people. Obviously, people seeing a monkey glancing through a magazine would quickly forget about paintings. Having piqued the guests' interest and drawn them to her, Woo would snap the magazine shut—keeping one foot stuck in as page marker—"clasp her hands around her tummy, rock back and forth" and appear to be dying laughing at their gullibility. Then, as soon as one of the onlookers smiled or said something to her, Woo would indulge in a primate version of coyly batting her eyelashes and showing herself so responsive that others came into the room to see what was going on, adding to the crowd and eventually drawing the one person she cared about, Carr, in to see what all the fuss was about. Mission accomplished—and Woo was happy again.[143]

During a camping trip with Carr, Pearson had gotten into some kind of noxious weed, possibly stinging nettle, causing a rash that spread from her hands to her face. As Carr carefully applied a salve to Pearson's skin, Woo sat nearby, intently watching her being doctored. Some days later, Carr and Pearson returned from an errand to an alarming sight: Woo had applied a salve to her own hands and face, but in this case the only available ointment she could find was a tube of Carr's green paint. "We had a green monkey for days," recalled Pearson. The incident was seen as both amusing and annoying, as the paint was everywhere and took effort to clean up, not least from Woo's pelt. But for Woo, was this not simply an act of gaining the attention she saw Pearson receive from Carr as she treated the young Carol's hands and face with ointment? Did Woo see Carr's paints as something more than colour, something peculiarly special because Carr spent so much time with them, spread them and mixed them, depended on them in combination as Woo depended on the combined attention, caring and occasional displays of anger that were the sum of a mother's love? I think that is closer to the truth.[144]

Woo was like any primate bonded to a human in her possessiveness of Emily Carr. But unlike the average monkey, who might bare teeth, cry out and even lash out physically at the person or animal who comes too close to that bonded individual, she proved she had developed sophisticated tactics not unlike those of a human child who knows how to gain attention. Pearson puts a finger on the crux of the Woo–Carr dynamic. All of Carr's animal family jockeyed for this attention, to be as close to her as they could get. But Carr seemed to realize that Woo was a special case, even more so than her dogs or birds, and so made certain to include her in everything she did, within reason. Like an indulged child—for such is how Carr treated her, if one can also imagine such a privileged child spending her life chained to a ring most of the day—Woo was normally provided that proximity and the liberties it implied, including, on at least one occasion, endlessly pestering Carr in a taxi cab until she allowed Woo to hold her brand-new hat. After all the fuss, the monkey sat quietly with the hat, as if through contact with this inanimate object, a mother's love could be accessed and enjoyed by mere touch. If Carr loved to hold wild things, Woo seemed to derive a similar joy touching their very opposite, so long as they were things that seemed to matter to Carr.[145]

Woo was clearly fascinated with the colours Carr used in the process of art making. Paint was another of those invisible ties that bound Woo to Carr, though we may imagine that the monkey found something disturbing, threatening, about their significance to the artist. What else had she seen, since the day she was brought to Hill House, but walls stacked or hung with flat squares and rectangles on which Carr had placed brushes full of this mysterious substance that, in Carr's hand, could make patterns and schemes and multicoloured atmospheres out of nothing? How often, sitting chained in the studio watching Carr at her easel, or in a tree below which Carr sat sketching, had Woo wondered about the process that turned her human mother's attention so fiercely toward that blank square or rectangle, to those tubes from which came colours squeezed onto a palette and tasted, one at a time and sometimes two or three together, by the brush, which lay them across a nothing that became a something?

Richard Natoli-Rombach, who had worked with the famous American primatologist Dian Fossey in Rwanda in 1974, recalled for me similar actions by Fossey's rescued golden lion tamarin, Kima. Fossey told Natoli-Rombach that she'd found Kima being offered for sale, took her as if to purchase her, and then never paid—her way of giving the finger, as it were, to the trade in wildlife. But like all monkeys, Kima needed constant attention, and in the real world there is no way for a busy human to provide that, particularly for Fossey. So Natoli-Rombach became the focus of Kima's attention. She first got to him by making an opening in his hut's grass matting roof. "My first sight of her," he recalled, "was seeing a monkey's head upside down over my bed." Kima began to make herself comfortable and, in so doing, ate anything she could find, including the type of non-comestibles Woo went after: glue, wood alcohol, matches, "the unthinkable," said Natoli-Rombach. One especially tantalizing object in his hut was a can of white pepper. "She was determined to get the top off," he recalled. "When I would warn her by the intonation of her name she would pretend to be looking out the window. What she was attempting to do is deceive me by pretending she was doing something else entirely. There is a behaviour in humans and other species that is called displacement behaviour where one behaviour is displaced by another so as to avoid exhibiting the original behaviour. Though I think her behaviour went well above displacement behaviour and was meant to deceive me regarding the intent of her actions." Natoli-Rombach pointed out that displacement activity seems to take place when an animal is unable to carry out a behaviour in which it has a vital interest and motivation. That would include an inability to be as close to the object of affection as the animal would like.[146]

In March 1930, Woo did more than just smear green paint on her face as ointment. She nearly killed herself.

Over the course of several days that month, Carr had been busy working on what was her only public address (a discourse on modern art at the Crystal Garden, a public conservatory located behind the Empress hotel). The idea for this lecture had been brought to Carr's attention by a woman who insisted she make the presentation before the notoriously conservative Women's Canadian Club (Carr's recollection was actually that the lady wished to "rub [the club women's] noses on canvases whether they like it or not"), to take place in tandem with Carr's first one-person show in Victoria. Carr was keen to share her considerable knowledge of modern art, though a public forum was, for her, a frightening place in which to do so.[147]

Zoologist Desmond Morris has pointed out that a cage is no place for a monkey, but that there is little recourse when a monkey is kept in a household environment, in which, uncontrolled, they can cause all kinds of damage to the human domestic setting, and injure their human keepers and themselves in the process.[148] In fact, soon after Woo had come to Hill House, she had developed a habit of picking at wall plaster, penetrating to the tough lathe as she dug one hole after another in the studio and elsewhere. "Woo's investigations were never superficial," Carr remarked.[149] As a result, Carr had to screw a ring into a section of wall, probably panelled in the thick matchboard she used throughout the house, in a corner of the studio, and attach Woo's chain to it, to keep her from doing further damage. Woo's cage had a sliding door "that was almost never locked," recalled Carol Pearson. Even had she opened the door and got out, Pearson wrote, "her chain kept her in one spot."[150]

Apart from the obvious problems with keeping a wild animal like a monkey in a domestic setting, a common criticism made by primate specialists is that monkeys need far more personal attention than they are likely to receive. And in the flurry to prepare for her talk, Carr had obviously not given Woo the attention she required. Carr hated speaking in public, and it can easily be imagined that, while writing came easily to her, her fears were holding thoughts hostage. And so, as she sat hunched over a table, pencil making little progress across the page, and wondering whether, when she did get the speech written, she could deliver it, Woo quietly opened the paint box, took out a tube of yellow paint and squeezed it into her mouth.

Vomiting bright daffodil over the carpet, furniture and herself, Woo got Carr's attention, and then some.

Carr abandoned her speech writing and spent the rest of the day alternately forcing emetics down the monkey, washing her, and sitting with her prone body across her knees, a hot-water bottle pressed to Woo's yellowed furry stomach. Carr called a veterinarian, who only added to her anxiety by informing her there was nothing more to be done and that it was doubtful the monkey would survive the night. In the middle of this crisis, the woman who had sponsored Carr's lecture telephoned for an update. Carr told her she could not possibly make the event if Woo got worse or died, and then had to argue with her when the sponsor refused to take this as sufficient justification for cancellation.

After a sleepless night on the part of Carr and Woo, by morning, the monkey had used up another of her lives, and proved to be not only breathing but seeming likely to do so for some time yet. Only then was Carr willing to leave her, still stained with what Vincent van Gogh saw as the colour of love, and go forth to speak to the Women's Canadian Club.

It's worth noting that this occasion, which almost didn't happen thanks to one of Carr's animals, did happen thanks to another. At the Crystal Garden, Carr, suddenly frozen before her audience, was unable to speak until griffon Ginger Pop broke away from the friend who was holding him, ran up to the dais and sat at Carr's feet. The artist was seen to relax, grow more comfortable and then proceed to give a talk that is as enlightening to us now as it was at the time it was given.[151]

With Woo's close call likely very much in her mind, Carr ended her talk with reference to her. She described her early fear of monkeys, her effort to allay it by visiting the London Zoo and looking them "fairly and squarely in the face." Do the same with modern art, Carr advised. Now that she had a monkey herself, "she has brought all kinds of fun into my life ... do think of my monkey and remember that tastes can be acquired." (Including, presumably, a taste for yellow paint.)[152]

Perhaps for similar reasons, on a camping expedition three years later, Woo gave an encore. To relieve herself of the rigours of travelling with boxes of animals, art supplies and food, requiring exhausting preparation at either end, in summer 1933 Carr purchased a used wood and canvas caravan. The van, which had already done much service on the roads of British Columbia, was rectangular in shape with the bowed top of a "travellers' wagon," with a door at one end and a section on one side that lifted into an awning. Carr dubbed it "the Elephant" in reference to its "gray and lumbering" bulk.[153] Packed with all she needed for its inaugural journey, along with dogs, Susie the rat and Woo, the Elephant was towed by one of Carr's friends to the woods of Goldstream Flats, the wooded provincial park situated between Victoria and the steep rise of the Malahat summit. Carr described it as "a narrow lowness where Goldstream babbles its way out to the Saanich Inlet on Finlayson Arm." It was a favourite spot, for Woo as well as for Carr.[154]

That day, there had been several visitors to the van, along with noisy picnic-seekers and their children parking nearby, people who stopped to talk to Carr, who then had to stop painting and be social. Carr had already noted how the monkey, who enjoyed bathing in the Goldstream River where there were exposed tree roots for her to dig in and climb through, was seen to hide as soon as day trippers appeared, which they frequently did, to camp and fish near Carr's spot. Often perfect strangers were drawn by the presence of the animals, most often by Woo. One of these visitors, Carr noted, professed to adore Woo despite her aloofness. Woo, in return, only scowled.[155]

During one of these social hours, while Carr was preoccupied in the van preparing food and drink, Woo grabbed a blob of green paint off her palette—green, significantly, being an especially pervasive colour in most of Carr's paintings. And again Woo swallowed that other enemy, pigment—or was it a beloved but impossibly distant friend?—the mysterious substance crucial to the act of art making that robbed the monkey of Carr's uninterrupted attention. Woo then proceeded to scamper up to Carr and cough the paint up. Carr rushed to the retching monkey, got her ruined dress off, used Epsom salts on and in her, rinsed out her cheeks till the green ran clear and then held her on her lap, as she had done before, to soothe her aching stomach. Woo was not so sickly she couldn't defend her hard-won territory: when the dogs came near, she had the strength to screech them away to a more agreeable distance. Carr chalked this anger up to Woo's sore stomach.[156] But was there not some self-satisfaction in that roar? Children who want attention will do much the same thing. On a more serious level of need, human children and adults will resort to self-harm. Eating paint, which had made her sick before, could be categorized as a self-harming act. But by these painful means had Woo, as before, achieved what she most desired, physical proximity to Carr, for which she was willing to pay any price? If this tells us about how much Woo loved, does it also tell us about how much more of Carr Woo wished she had?

"Miss Carr taught me a lot about animals," wrote Carol Pearson, "about their thinking, habits, their loving; their very deep trust and respect; how one has to strive to attain it; and the value of it once it is yours."[157] "How delightful it is," Carr wrote, "when animals stay near you for the joy and pleasure of your company, not because they must."[158]

Carr knew she stood for everything in their personal worlds. She gave them food and shelter; without her, the monkey, dogs, cat, birds and rat could not have survived, so indeed they knew they must stay near her. Yet the artist was aware that there were deeper emotions going on than just the pang of hunger at dinnertime. "One is so obviously their God," she wrote, "that it ought to make one careful." How terrible would it be, she reasoned, if one got to heaven and found God "snappy and cross"?[159] Carr took Woo and her other animals seriously, as she believed they did her, and tried to be everything she assumed they believed her to be—almost a god. But did Woo get enough of her? Could Woo have ever got enough? This power over the animals whose presence formed the very foundation of Carr's personal and artistic life would lend her decisions on their behalf a sort of horrible irony. Because as she would learn, as even deities need to do, there is a heartbreak that comes with authority over life and death in the awful power love gives. One that no human can hand over to a deity to shoulder. One that haunts as long as love and memory last.

CHAPTER 7

The Last Summer

Woo's last camping trip in the Elephant with Carr took place in September 1936. There was no particular reason to assume it would be the last, because at this point the sixty-four-year-old Carr's life was starting a slow but invigorating upswing. If 1927, the year Carr's work was exhibited at the National Gallery in Ottawa, leading to wider exposure and her life-changing meeting with Lawren Harris of the Group of Seven, had been a major turning point for Carr as artist, the next five years had brought nationwide recognition not only as artist but as writer and would bring the art world of Canada and numerous admirers from around the world to her modest Victoria doorstep.

Carr was not fond of change, yet she knew she needed it now. She had put Hill House on the market, and by the spring of 1937, she could be happy that she and the animals had survived the sale of and move from Simcoe Street, where Carr had lived since 1913. The property was sold partly in order to pay off debts, but also because it was clear Carr could no longer physically carry out her duties as a landlady. As Dr. Phyllis Marie Jensen wrote, "it was not because of the people contact but the unending tiring responsibility of catering to others when she wanted to be painting and tramping in the woods with her dogs."[160] Giving up her day job would allow Carr the long-desired freedom to pursue her artistic endeavours without distraction.

To prepare for the sale, Carr went about Hill House filling in all the holes in plaster and gouges in wood created by Woo's active fingers. In what seems a desperate bid to sever herself from her past, she burned countless drawings and paintings, letters and photographs and memorabilia, in the back garden. "I want to cry but I have no tears," Carr wrote in her journal. By March, her work was done. "I have slipped out of the chemise of worry that 646 Simcoe dressed me in," she said.[161] What she did not realize is that in taking off this old troubling garment, she would don another, newer one, without knowing it at the time or divining how soon it too would begin to weigh on her.

Carr moved to a cottage at 316 Beckley Street, now Beckley Avenue (the cottage's place taken years ago by a condominium complex) in what was then a working-class district. It was a neighbourhood she came to love and indeed feel more comfortable in than she ever had at 646 Simcoe. "These folk live more," she wrote.[162]

Her reputation as artist and eccentric pet lady preceded her, as described by Bert Hudson, who was a boy when Carr moved next door to his parents' home. It was one thing to see her vivid canvases, hundreds of them, being carted into the cottage, in a neighbourhood where fine art was something that happened somewhere else, and to see her menagerie carried or walked up to the porch. But it was another thing altogether to see Carr, herself the most colourful new addition to the neighbourhood. According to Bert, she made him think of a snowman or a portly hausfrau encased in a busy plaid smock, stern braids encircling her head, her cheeks suntanned and those piercing eyes looking at, and apparently through, everything she beheld. But it was Carr's animals, not her art, that Bert was looking for through his mother's curtains. He was to see plenty of them soon enough.[163]

His elder sister Phyllis was the brave one at first, visiting Carr and bringing back tales of what life was like in her mysterious household. From this we get a rare outsider glimpse of what Carr gave Woo to eat. Phyllis related to Bert how, on one occasion, Carr served kippers for dinner. Phyllis watched her give a whole kipper to Woo, who cleaned every bone. She also described Woo's passion for lettuce, which Carr bought for her by the head. In time, Bert gradually came to be trusted enough to look after the animals when

Carr was away. Bert noticed how suspicious they were even then, refusing to take food from anyone except Carr. He noted that while he was able to finally get on the dogs' good side, such was never to be the case with Woo; and while the dogs never bit him, Woo, he claimed, gnashed her teeth at him more often then not. It was only thanks to good luck, he added, and the nimbleness of youth that he was able to put in an order for four beers with one hand without having to use the fingers of both.[164]

Carr was happy that her animal family was taking the enormous change so well. Thanks to the cottage's compact size and windows in rooms all round, her dogs had the special double pleasure of always finding a square of sunshine to lie in and to be able to see Carr from almost any vantage point. Woo, though now about fifteen years of age and putting on weight, was excited to the point of frenzy, hopping in her cage, "very rambunctious, screeching and banging," Carr wrote approvingly.[165]

Trips in the Elephant at this time seemed to be similarly full of a happiness that neither Carr nor her animals had previously known to this degree. There was less need to strive, more freedom to savour. "Country smells are sweeter and wilder, more subtle and mysterious and evasive," Carr wrote.[166] On this last trip, with just herself and her animal family, she sketched, sang to the dogs. She noted, as she sang, having no confidence her voice was worth hearing even to the animal world, how her dogs and monkey gazed up at her, as if in wonder at her effort if not her artistry. "They take it for what it is worth," she said. When it was too wet to leave the van, Carr played This Little Piggy on Woo's toes and fingers.[167]

Carr, too, was learning to take things for what they were worth. Lizzie's death in August, though a blow of enormous proportions to a woman who had always known this sister as a kind of maternal force of nature, could not dampen the beauties of that September in the Elephant. Carr looked at the passing of Lizzie, and of Hill House, philosophically, recalling once seeing a chained bird in England struggle so violently to free itself that it succeeded only by leaving one leg, wrenched off in the struggle, behind. "Has one always to lose something, a very part of them," she wondered, "to gain freedom?" The answer appeared to be yes.[168]

Sadly, Carr little reckoned, writing these words, how much she would have to relinquish in just four months' time.

Carr seems to have understood for some while already that she did not possess a healthy heart. For years, as she wrote in her journal, she had experienced "pain that has come and gone intermittently."[169] Aside from her inability to stay safely above the emotional turmoil of running an apartment house, and suffering consequent nervous storms, Carr also smoked heavily, and likely didn't eat what would be considered a balanced diet. Slender as a girl, she had begun to put on weight at the sanatorium over thirty years before, and had not been able to get rid of it.

And the new year of 1937 began with more stress than her heart could take. Two days in, Carr grew frustrated beyond proportion when British-born Canadian painter Jack Shadbolt was late coming to see her recent work—she had told him to come early as she had sketches to post to Lawren Harris. This delayed them getting out. The visit ended with Carr in a peevish mood, sharing her critique of Shadbolt in her journal and getting in a jab at the "bunch over there in Vancouver" who didn't understand forests any better than he did. She also had a moment of the kind of depthless self-doubt that continued to haunt her for the rest of her life when she confessed, "Or am I a doddering old fool weakly toddling round my grave's brink … ?"[170]

In the bitter temperatures of January 9, Carr began suffering pains in her chest. They came, as they had done before. This time, they did not go away. After hours of agony in body and mind, Carr finally called a doctor. The man's rather obvious diagnosis was that she was suffering from heart trouble, and his tame prescription seems to have been that she not lift anything or bend over. Waiting impatiently on her bed, or sitting when she would rather have been doing something, Carr described trying hard to overcome what was happening to her body, slipping out of herself to float into the trees. But for Emily Carr, sitting in one place, and being told to do so, went against the grain of everything she was. She probably did not obey the doctor's orders, even while he was still in the house.

Next day, the pain and fear were worse. The doctor arrived again, gave her a sedative and adjured her again to lie quietly. Carr slept, but when she awoke, she had the pains again, and with them came the frustration of being unable to look after her animals and house. She couldn't have done so even had she tried, for she was drugged and dizzy. Luckily she had help; unluckily, it was not the help she most needed. Mrs. Hudson from next door was joined by Carr's sister Alice, and as so often happens when others come to assist a patient, invasion rather than peacefulness was the initial atmosphere they created. The cottage was in chaos. Woo, unable to see Carr, screeched at the women from her cage in the kitchen, and the dogs ran away every time Alice or Mrs. Hudson tried to catch one of them. The dogs finally jumped on the bed and fought each other on top of Carr, and the women tried to control them as Carr wept, struggling between her heart's pain and her heart's love. It may have been at this moment, when Alice, who had spent years trying to make Carr behave, who knew her weaknesses all too well, concluded that the animals were a large part of Carr's problem, and began to think of ways to remove them. This is a scenario all too familiar in our era, in which companion animals of the aged are often sent to shelters when their guardians are placed in a care facility. They too often go, like Carr's animals, from the warm and familiar to a world of uncertainty, fear and in high-kill shelters, death if nobody adopts them.[171]

Carr was moved to Victoria's St. Joseph's Hospital, a four-storey brick structure dating from 1908 that still sits across the street from the broad gardens of St. Ann's Academy. There, in delirium, she thought she saw nurses fluttering about her like butterflies. Unable to do anything, Carr lay prone, weeping as she contemplated a crucifix on the wall opposite, its silver Christ body appearing to shimmer even in shadow.

A few days later, in that room, on January 21, Carr took a pen and paper and began to write a letter. It was sent to Nan Cheney, a friend in Vancouver. Carr offered Cheney her griffons, Tantrum and Vanathe. They were, as she told her that spring, her last sire and dam who were "supposed to hold up the glory of the tribe." Cheney took them gladly, but their fate was sealed in a less happy way. Within three months, both dogs were dead from distemper.[172]

The dogs, Carr wrote later, had at least been easy enough to find homes for. "Few people," she wrote, "want to bother with a monkey."[173] So she wrote another letter. This one was to the Stanley Park Zoo.

The man to whom she addressed her letter was the keeper of the Monkey House, someone she said she had known for some time. In fact, he may well have been the same man whom she had met to discuss bringing Woo to the Monkey House years earlier, to breed her with a male macaque.[174] Now Carr asked the keeper to take Woo. The keeper did not have authority to accept an animal on his own, but Carr claimed she received approval from the Vancouver Park Board itself; we have to take her word for this, as due to the fact that I could not locate the minutes for January through March 1937, there is no evidence the board did agree. All we know is that arrangements were made for Woo to be taken to the zoo before Carr was released from hospital, and that Woo was no longer living at 316 Beckley Street when Carr was brought back home from St. Joseph's.

The day she wrote her letter to the zookeeper, Carr angrily and mysteriously noted in her journal that she had received a visit from a doctor who "told me too much." What was this new "brutal telling" about? Had the doctor given a medical prognosis that shocked her? Had he cautioned her that she could no longer live as she had been doing, and that her animals, which according to medical opinion she could no longer safely care for, must go?

Carr had had several other visitors at St. Joseph's who "told too much," among them Alice. Carr knew that Alice was not in her element caring for her animals. Indeed, Alice constantly conveyed to Carr what a burden it was for her to look after them *and* come to the hospital to see her sister on top of everything else she was doing. We don't know what happened, or whether anything happened, as it pertains to Woo. We don't know whether Alice—who was herself having health issues, including encroaching blindness—said something to the doctor, or said something to Carr directly, or nothing to anybody. But it cannot be denied that if anyone was capable of taking action when it came to Carr's animals and, specifically, to sending Woo away, Alice as next of kin was the person who would have been in the best position to authorize these significant alterations to Emily's household.

A friend of Carr's, Willie Newcombe, who would later serve in the important capacity of packing and shipping Carr's paintings after her health crisis predictably raised widespread interest in her work, was given the task of finding homes for the animal companions left over after the surplus griffons were removed. Carr could not face doing so, and in any case was in no condition to undertake this sad responsibility.[175]

The once happy little cottage on Beckley Street became a locus of sadness virtually overnight. One of Carr's pets seemed to know the end was near. While she was at St. Joseph's, her rooster, Cocky Do, suddenly died. Cocky Do had been among her closest animal family; he would sit on her chest and chortle "softly with his head bent down on you, as if he was absolving you of all your sins," wrote Carr. In a way, he absolved her (and those making these decisions for her) by leaving before he could be got rid of.[176]

Cocky Do's exit was easy, by comparison. After letters and phone calls, the remaining animals seem to have found homes, some on a temporary basis, some for good. Of all Carr's griffons (Ginger Pop had died some years before), Pout remained, but not at the cottage; until her return from hospital, Pout was sent away to be looked after until Carr was better able to care for the dog. That Carr was very much not a part of the decision-making process where her animals were concerned is evident in her worried resignation to never seeing Pout again, though she in fact did get him back later.[177]

As for the monkey, Willie "nailed her into a box, gave her into strange hands," was all Carr knew. "When I came home she was gone."[178]

Swiss biologist Dr. Heini Hediger, who wrote about wild animals in captivity, explained his view: that capturing a wild animal and placing it in a cage is to destroy the only world it knows and offer it another with which it cannot negotiate.[179] Never having known freedom, an animal born in captivity would not have the same grave task ahead of it, rebuilding that ruined structure, but even so, whatever constituted its captivity was its world, and to alter that was to accomplish virtually the same destruction. How Woo reacted to this destruction of her world is part of her enduring mystery. Her screeching in the kitchen, as Alice and other of Carr's friends and neighbours tripped over themselves looking after the ailing artist, with Carr weeping helplessly on her bed, is probably as much as we would want to imagine. Willie, whom she knew but whom she probably did not consider any more a friend than she did Bert Hudson, grappled with Woo and put her, screeching and fighting, into the crate. She had not been in one, readied for shipping somewhere, since an infant some fourteen years earlier, first for the sail from Java to California, then for the sail from San Francisco to Victoria, then dumped together with others who bullied her, finally rescued by a kind woman who made for her the only home she had known. And now, Woo was back where she had begun. "No bars of asylum or jails or poverty or sickness or any devilishness whatever can arrest the flight of our imaginings," wrote Carr, with sad knowledge of what she spoke, "nor hide from us what is stored in our memories."[180] Woo's memories must surely have been hectically relived as her crate was loaded onto a truck and driven to the ferry dock, lifted into the hold of the ferry, rocked and bumped for the sail across the strait, lifted onto another vehicle and driven through twists and turns, noise and confusion of a strange city, into the tall trees of Stanley Park, and its zoo.

For Woo, too, presumably nothing could arrest the flight of *her* imaginings on this fearful journey, to a place she had never been for what devilishness she could not know.

CHAPTER 8

The Monkey House

Stanley Park Zoo got its start in 1888 with an errant and irreverent bear cub.

The man who is officially considered the park's first ranger, Henry Avison (Sr.), a young Irish immigrant with a neat moustache, captured the cub. Ranger Avison's son, Henry Jr., recalled how the bear was chained to a tree stump, within reach of any onlooker foolhardy enough to approach it, until the incautious wife of a church reverend decided to jab it with her umbrella. The bear swiped at her with its claws, ripping off part of her dress (as well as, we may assume, a large part of her dignity).[181]

When a Stanley Park commissioner, shocked by this incident, called for the bear's destruction, Mrs. Avison, the former Kate Gray of Edinburgh, refused. "She handled the bears herself; no one else would go near them," said Henry Jr., pointing out that his mother was the young zoo's first keeper. This close call was why, soon afterward, the bear pit was built, into which photos from the period show visitors to the nascent zoo looking down from behind a secure fence. Even that long ago, said Henry Jr. in a 1933 interview, "the animals consisted of some monkeys, some coon, the bears—eight cages in all, all wooden."[182] There was even music—albeit of the blaring kind—courtesy of the Vancouver City Band, its presence making the zoo a kind of open-air circus, one where the animals didn't leap through flaming hoops at the crack of a master's whip but nervously paced their cages, out of time with the beat, under the equally controlling gaze of the public.[183]

The establishment of zoos like the one in Stanley Park was inspired by a fascination with collections of exotic things—peculiar possessions popular in most eras but truly endemic to the Victorian age. Along with other distant colonies, subdued through militant Christianity or guns or both, British Victorians loved to gather and display objects, whether vases and porcelain cupids or glassware or, as did many who went abroad to Asia or Africa, tribal masks, Egyptian tomb knick-knacks, and the pelts and taxidermied figures of animals they had hunted or purchased from hunters. No upper-class Victorian parlour was complete without something like a lion-skin rug under the grand piano. Wildness and exoticism had their place in the otherwise highly civilized domestic interior.

Of course, living animals were even more desirable.

Writing of Cairo's zoo, founded in the late nineteenth century, historian Alan Mikhail noted that the menagerie's collection "was built through colonial ventures of animal capture"—an apt description of the organization of any public zoo from the Victorian period. Like Cairo's, Vancouver's zoo was no less an example of the period's "defining features ... commodification; empire; separation," which had replaced an earlier attitude toward menageries as sources of "intimacy, co-operation, utility [and] wonder."[184]

The function of a late Victorian zoo was supported by the moral uplift of a claim to serve as education for the populace, along with lucrative entertainment opportunities provided by a popular public concession. Even human beings were displayed in zoos in this period—including dark-skinned people, as symbolic as the animals alongside them of the triumph of white Christian dominion over every creeping thing, to quote that popular Victorian text, the Bible.

By the time Woo arrived in 1937, the Stanley Park Zoo, though popular with the public, seemed far more headache than boon for Park Board commissioners. It wasn't just the ongoing challenge of caring for the animals, though more attention should have been paid to this than evidently was done. A public space brings its own onerous issues. Even in what we know to have been, compared to our current period in history, the far less litigious world of the Depression era, incensed Vancouver parents were writing threatening letters to the board to complain of injuries when their children fell while playing in the park. In a singular instance, when the son of Frank W. Linnington tripped on a tree root, Linnington Sr. wrote a letter to the Park Board, demanding fifty dollars for doctor's fees—this, in Depression-era 1933, amounted to several hundred dollars in today's currency. The board paid the demand, no questions asked.[185] When boys did more than trip over their own feet but thrust hands into the cages in the Monkey House, made possible by unobstructed access and apparent lack of oversight from staff, and ran away screaming when a finger was bitten, again, the board paid up: the customer was always right.[186]

A year before young Linnington found himself surprised by tree roots in a forest, the board, which did not need to seek consensus for these payouts, found itself divided on the care of the animals under its jurisdiction, and in one case adjudicated an issue that could have been settled quickly via common business sense.

The Vancouver SPCA, founded in the city of New Westminster in 1898, had been alerted to the poor conditions of the zoo, and its board had sent a letter about this to the commissioners.[187] The SPCA offered the sum of twenty-five dollars—no small amount in 1932—for badgers, bobcats and a lynx they had confirmed were being kept in substandard conditions. This offer, entirely beneficial to the zoo, touched a nerve in two of the commissioners, James Fyfe-Smith and Edgar George Bayne, who motioned abruptly "that the animals in question be destroyed." Ultimately an amendment carried to the effect the board try to sell the animals in question, and if this could not be carried out by the end of the year, then the animals should be euthanized. As this meeting took place on December 9, that left a little less than a month to literally buy time for the animals, but it kept park rangers and their guns temporarily at bay.[188]

There is no indication whether homes were found for them, but there was another urgent topic in the SPCA's complaint. In addition to drawing attention to the badgers, bobcats and lynx, the SPCA pointed out that the zoo's monkeys were not receiving proper feeding, nor were they being inadequately protected from the public. In that meeting's minutes, the topic of the health of the inhabitants of the Monkey House was not addressed at all.

In the matter of this total silence as to the primates' welfare, we might think it understandable that the Park Board members could not possibly have had time to concern themselves with the inhabitants of every cage and enclosure in the zoo—as we've seen, it is obvious from the way at least two board members reacted to the SPCA's complaint about the badgers, bobcats and lynx that the best way to deal with these annoying creatures was to put them to death at once. How, then, could they be expected to bother with every criticism of the way animals were housed and fed?

But visualize this: the Park Board commissioners were not meeting in a drawing room in a distant wealthy suburb of the city. They convened for business on the second floor of the Stanley Park Pavilion, a wood and stone structure that first opened in 1913. The pavilion is located within a few paces and, depending on intervening trees and foliage in 1932, possibly within sight of the Monkey House itself. Did anyone from the board walk over the rise, pop a head in the Monkey House and check on its inhabitants? The Park Board minutes' lips are sealed.[189]

In 1928, death came to the Monkey House in a particularly violent fashion.

A brown male rhesus macaque had been given to the zoo in 1927—ten years before Woo's arrival—by a Mr. G. Martin, and was dubbed by the keepers with the bluntly racist name "Hogan's Alley," after an area of Vancouver that was the nucleus of the city's African-Canadian community. (Roughly the equivalent of naming a monkey "Harlem" in the United States.)

While feeding the monkeys in March of the following year, a keeper named David Keddie had an altercation with Hogan's Alley. To read the Vancouver *Province*'s breathless coverage, one would think a great ape the size of a silverback gorilla had jumped the man:

"a huge beast presented to the park last year," the monkey "flew at the keeper's throat," then sank its "fangs" into Keddie's wrist. Keddie "pounded it about the head with his right fist," screaming for help. He then fell, and Hogan's Alley escaped the Monkey House and headed for the trees of Stanley Park. While Keddie was rushed to hospital, his wounds apparently so painful he had to be given anaesthetic just to put a dressing on his wrist, a hunt was already being planned for Hogan's Alley: "A posse of keepers armed with rifles and shotguns was organized."[190]

The monkey was not long for freedom. The *Vancouver Sun* reported next day that the "little plain brown monkey, known as 'Hogan's Alley' ... was shot at dusk on Tuesday." The monkey was spotted sitting on the roof of a shed, and park policeman Sidney Wilson was summoned with his gun: "It required three shotgun shells and two revolver bullets to kill the animal."[191]

At least the *Sun* bothered to point out to its readers that Hogan's Alley was no man-killing monster, but a "little plain brown monkey"—yet nobody seems to have raised the question: Why did the monkey attack Keddie? "While it had not shown a disposition to be friendly," wrote the *Province*, "it was not suspected of being vicious."[192] How then were the monkeys treated by their keepers? In particular, how was Hogan's Alley treated, and did abuse lead to the "unexpected" attack?

This lends some background to the Monkey House. It was to this place, which the Vancouver SPCA had complained about to the body in charge of overseeing the monkeys who lived there, that Carr sent Woo to live in 1937.

Built in 1907–08, the Monkey House—which stood within sight of the children's playground that is still in situ today—was designed by W.H. Archer, who was responsible for various mansions designed for wealthy Vancouverites as well as simpler houses of worship (from the red-walled Gothic gem of St. Paul's Anglican Church in the West End to a long-vanished Buddhist temple in Chinatown).[193] A high rectangle with hip roof and a raised ridge vent, and constructed at a total cost of $7,500, the Monkey House was one of the most expensive structures in Stanley Park. One-third of that cost went to the boiler installed to heat the structure, which housed not just monkeys (there were ten of them in 1911) but a variety of tropical birds.[194]

When her crate was opened and light spilled in, Woo would have found herself in a situation foreign in just about every respect. It was winter and bitterly cold. The boiler's heat may have helped compensate to a degree. But in the Monkey House, Woo would have no more pinafores to wear, no familiar stove to sit by. No more dog companions. Just an environment utterly strange to her, filled with monkeys who frightened her and birds who were not the ones she had known at home. And no more Emily Carr.

We know from Carr's writings and accounts of others who visited the monkey that Woo, unlike the other residents, was kept in her own cage in the Monkey House. Had Carr urged the keeper to house her separately, knowing that Woo did not mix well with other monkeys? Or did the keeper place Woo with the others, witness some unhappy results, then move her to what amounted to an isolation cell, for her own safety but leaving her both traumatized and segregated? We don't know the details. But there she lived, within sight and hearing of the other monkeys.

In this cage, Woo, who feared them, was exposed to human strangers on a daily basis. Her first winter in Stanley Park must have been all the more difficult due to the weather, which was extreme. In fact, the winter of 1937 was one of the coldest recorded in the province's history of meteorological record keeping. There had always been problems ensuring the zoo's animals did not freeze in winter. As early as 1907, records tell of extraordinary efforts to try to keep the animals warm enough for survival. "The ranger boarded up enclosures," wrote environmental historian Sean Kheraj, "and lit fires to protect vulnerable animals during snowfalls and cold snaps." As we've seen, keeping the monkeys warm enough was still a problem in the early 1930s, before Woo arrived.[195]

As for the day-to-day reality of Woo's life at Stanley Park Zoo, we can only guess. The only other fact about Woo of which we can be certain is that in January 1938, a year later, she was still alive at the zoo, because Carr referred to her in a letter. "Do go to the Park Zoo," Carr asked her friend Nan Cheney that month, "and kiss 'Woo' for me. I would love to see her."[196] We also know, because Carr refers to it in her writing, that her friends did come to visit the monkey each Sunday, bringing her familiar treats and familiar faces. Edythe Hembroff-Schleicher was one of these. She later wrote that when she visited Woo in 1938, the monkey, whom she was accustomed to seeing dressed in her pinafore, seemed strangely more naked than the other monkeys. Though Woo appeared in healthy enough condition, Hembroff-Schleicher noted that she behaved in an anxious manner, quite unlike her, throwing herself from one side of the cage to the other. And Woo did not seem to know who her visitor was, though she had spent a good deal of time with Hembroff-Schleicher in the recent past. It is hard to deny that of all the places where Woo could have been, the Monkey House at the Stanley Park Zoo was the worst possible choice.[197]

How incapacitated was Carr at the time Woo was sent away? It's a reasonable question, because by 1938, according to a letter Nan Cheney wrote to Eric Brown of the National Gallery two months later, Carr is mentioned as already having two dogs, along with an unspecified number of chipmunks and birds to look after in the Beckley Street cottage. We have to wonder, if someone as ill as Carr was judged able to look after dogs—who needed frequent walking, at least in the garden if not down the street—why could she not have been allowed to keep a monkey, who spent most of her time chained to a wall and who was, by Carr's own admission, becoming less active with age?[198]

And Carr's formerly grave situation improved. Growing stronger after her enforced rest and bolstered by renewed interest in her work, Carr was finally able to get across the strait to Vancouver in fall 1938. But from this trip there is no extant mention of Woo. So we can assume that sometime after January of that year, and prior to Carr's visit in autumn, Woo had passed away.[199]

Carol Pearson, long married by 1938 and living in Ontario, wrote that Woo died of a broken heart a mere two weeks after arriving at Stanley Park Zoo. Pearson's grasp of chronology does not always match the charm of her recollections, which she wrote as an elderly woman residing on the other side of Canada, and in this she is clearly mistaken. But something in Pearson's diagnosis rings true, if only because Carr herself hinted at the same, albeit with a different chronology, in the final lines of her book *The Heart of a Peacock*:

> Woo lived in the Monkey house for a year. My friends went one Sunday and found her cage empty.
>
> "Old age—natural causes," said the keeper. "No ail, no mope … just died."
>
> "Fine exit, Woo! If that is monkey way, I am glad domesticity did not spoil it."[200]

Woo's death, at around age seventeen, could hardly be said to have been caused by old age. In the wild, and even in captivity, crab-eating macaques like Woo can live to be thirty, at least among those who are left to flourish in the matriarchal setting all female macaques are part of in the wild. A study by the University of Exeter, published in 2017, found that when female macaques are surrounded by female relatives, they tend to have a better chance at living a longer life than living in isolation.[201]

But Woo had no one. The sad truth may well be that so far as Woo's death was concerned, a life of unbroken proximity to the woman who had been her mother, rather than exile to a zoo, would likely have given her a much longer life and, certainly, a far happier end.

In the years following Woo's death, Carr recovered her health and flourished. Spurred on by increased interest in her work, Carr painted, sketched and wrote like never before. Tight planes of colour, loosening from the middle 1920s on, now billowed freely, rattling in the breeze of public attention and attracting notice from critics, galleries and buyers. Exhibitions followed, Carr's name went up in lights and on top of this she became, virtually overnight, a popular author.

Carr's first book, *Klee Wyck*, was published in 1941 and won the Governor General's Award. Several more books, each a mix of autobiography and creative nonfiction, bloomed under her pen. Some of these books were published after her death. One of these, *The Heart of a Peacock*, was not published until 1953. Among this book's fifty-one short chapters, Woo's biography occupies twenty-three of them, and Carr's telling of "Woo's Life" is her most detailed, crushingly poignant and raucously funny in what is arguably among her best pieces of prose.

It is clear that Carr knew how important the monkey had been to her—as an animal companion unlike any other, as a source of unpredictable joys and just as unpredictable crises, and as muse, though she does not credit her as such. We also know that in the final months of Carr's life, in 1945, Woo was very much on her mind.

That year, Carr was often bedridden, either in the cottage she shared with her sister Alice, or in hospital care. Among the work to which she was able to give her flagging energies, she had the strength to complete one last portrait of Woo. A life-size image of the monkey, the painting shows Woo squatting on a branch of an apple tree. Above her, a grey-barked trunk swoops, curves, terminates in jagged branches. Green fruit clusters here and there, lustrous as jade. Alongside this lustre there is an odd violence to the painting, as if it had begun as something calmer, with an intention to depict the quiet fructification of nature, only to have Woo leap into its centre, disturbing the equilibrium like a stone breaking the surface of a pool, showing that nature is not about standing still, that like art, Nature's greatness is all in the momentum.

This Woo could not be more different from the Woo of the early 1930s portrait, which Carr kept nearby where she could see it from her bed. That Woo stands quietly on her tree branch like a human child, wears her orange skirt as a child might and is looking intently at something outside the range of the viewer. Like a child mesmerized by a circus parade wending its way down some distant street, she could not care less who is watching her. The second Woo of 1945, however, is the monkey as Nature made her. She wears her pelt only, and she is the one gazing, boldly, this time straight back at the observer. Carr claimed Woo saved a special grin only for her, but it is not in evidence here. Is this an accusatory stare? Is this not so much Woo as a personification of Carr's guilt at having sent her away?

Yet as serious as the monkey appears to be, she is holding an apple, not for herself but, seemingly, for whoever had the best chance of taking it from her. A good friend to the Chinese community in Victoria, one who sympathetically tried to understand their art and their way of life, a white woman who deplored the racism to which Chinese-Canadians were subjected, did Carr know enough about Chinese symbolism to understand that an apple stands for peace? (The character for "apple," *ping*, sounds similar in pronunciation to the character for "peace.") Woo's mouth is green, as if she has tasted of the forbidden fruit she is offering to the spectator. Is this Woo making a peace offering to her human mother? Has Carr captured her own conflicted feelings about sending Woo to a place from which she did not return?[202]

If Woo's spirit seemed especially embedded in this portrait, she also haunted Carr's mind. A nurse who tended the artist toward the end told of how Carr murmured one word as she lay in delirium. It was Woo's name, over and over again, spoken, perhaps, with the same breathless apprehension that Woo herself had shown on finding herself in Carr's studio in 1923. Like Woo upon first entering Hill House, Carr too, as she lay delirious, was on the brink of a new chapter. And though death was the only destination on this ticket, it was nonetheless a beginning for Carr, just as it had been for Woo.

After Carr's death from a heart attack at the start of March 1945, Alice Carr made a kind of shrine of her sister's studio in the little schoolhouse they shared on St Andrew's Street in James Bay, ready for the visitors who soon came in droves. In a corner, set up to balance on the wainscot, much as the monkey herself may have tried to do, was Carr's portrait of Woo in the apple tree.[203]

Carr's grave in Ross Bay Cemetery, like Woo's in whatever unknown part of Vancouver her remains lie, was unmarked till, in 1963, the Victoria Historical Society placed a stone rectangle, engraved with the sober facts of her wild life, into the soil above her bones.

As for Woo, her memorial remains only in Carr's stories and letters and journals, in the two portraits she painted of her, and somewhere among the nodding pink and yellow blooms of the Stanley Park Rose Garden, founded a year before Woo's 1921 birth. There, like the fragrance of flowers unseen but appreciated, the ghosts of unhappy captives do not have to be seen to be felt, or to be believed.

PART II

Out of the silent wood,
As if from the closing door
Of another world and another lovelier mood,
Hear'st thou the hermit pour—
So sweet! so magical!—
His golden music, ghostly beautiful.

—Archibald Lampman, "The Bird and the Hour"

CHAPTER 9

Wild Things

"She came to understand her animals better after meeting them halfway in a No-man's-land she created," wrote Canadian art historian Maria Tippett, "where animals and humans achieved complete harmony."[204]

This statement encapsulates and celebrates everything that mattered in Carr's relationships with her animal family. But we must acknowledge that by today's standards, Emily Carr was not an ideal pet guardian. (Using those same standards, I avoid the word "owner.") We now have an opportunity of gaining a better perspective on the nonfictional aspects of that life, as opposed to the fairy tales, for Carr and for her animals.

As we've seen, the ineluctable need to hold wild things had a long history with Carr. While in East Anglia Sanatorium from 1903 to 1904, she was encouraged by her doctor to breed English songbirds, which Carr planned to import to Canada. To carry out this therapy, she had to rob whole birds' nests; and while feeding and caring for the young birds seems to have helped Carr recover from her breakdown, the project eventually had to be given up for practical reasons, and the birds, hand-fed and tame, were released to an uncertain fate. Even then, Carr does not seem to have given the situation much concern. She had achieved her satisfaction; now it was for nature to take its pitiless but just course.

Carr needed to possess, and there was love as well as collecting culture in that possession. But she was part of the tradition in which the *ethics* of possession simply don't apply—if this type of ethics, as uncommon in her time as expected in our own, had a place anywhere on the spectrum of awareness of anyone born in the Victorian period.

Carr liked to see herself as someone she never was—the stereotypical impassive "Indian," silent in the storm, adjusting to the exacting requirements of Earth without murmur, wise in choices, philosophical in outlook. Indigenous people, Carr believed, possibly thinking of her friend Sophie Frank, a Squamish woman who had lost nearly a dozen infants, faced death with ease, because death was a part of life. Carr may have perceived something similar in the way that the Indigenous people she knew seemed to react to the act of parting from someone they cared for. No love must be so deep that the loved one could not turn and walk away, for love's time was done, and the gods of Nature and the wise ancestors, are the ones in charge, not we. Carr herself was not really like that. She was a product of her time, and victim of it too. Brought up in the toughest tenets of a strain of Christianity the joylessness of which left her cold, to her, the only deity worthy of worship was the Earth herself, yet she was capable of shifting responsibility for her actions to a god when it suited her. As she grandly rationalized to Carol Pearson, "It is not so difficult to part with an animal we love when we remember it is dear to the heart of Him." This stoicism is a large part of her genius as artist—a bleak but clear-eyed acceptance of Nature's laws as she saw them, a refusal to sugar-coat reality as she perceived it. Carr's mature, finished artistic style has been too easily imitated by artists who, while not lacking her skill, possess none of her special ferocity. That ferocity was what she had always used to help her face life, just as it was what she used to explore the deepest, most dangerous, most inexplicable recesses of the natural world. Yet Carr, being human, had her limits. She may have conquered the fear that had paralyzed her artistic power. But she still had a heart that bled when it was cut. And so she was to find that when her own time came to shoulder the pain of parting from those she loved, there was no deity of Earth or of heaven to step in, no "Indian" alter ego to soften the blow for her.[205]

Throughout Carr's life, her sisters, though they in no way can be said to not have loved her, still managed to make her feel inadequate, misguided, ungodly. Given this, perhaps holding a "wild thing" justified and reinforced her own sense of being wild, a romantic changeling mistakenly left in the nest with a family of sedate missionaries, and who had to fly away to survive. No wonder Carr felt more at home with wild things, in wildness. Yet her problems, and those of the wild things, began when she brought them back to the human setting in which she lived, where they did not belong, hopelessly tangling them in a complicated net of alien human emotions and values.

The peacock of her eponymous collection of animal stories is one of the most heartbreaking examples, a tragic parable of what captivity and human dominance can do to an animal. Carr writes of this peacock, whom she had known in her youth. The bird lived in Beacon Hill Park, a descendant of escapees from the gardens of colonial Victorians who kept them in an effort to emulate the high style of English gentry. Carr wrote that the bird would often visit her father's garden and, in so doing, formed a bond with her. Carr loved the peacock for his loyalty, stating that his heart was even more beautiful than his feathers. His was also a heart more tender than many humans understood. Unfortunately, those charged with overseeing the park's peacocks complained about the bird's frequent absences without leave. Carr said this complaint reached the "City fathers, whose fatherly instructions were 'Pen the peacock.'"[206]

She went to visit the bird in his enclosure, where she saw members of the public clamouring at him to show his feathers. After all, was he not their property, and at their beck and call? She related, in a scene that has haunting echoes of Woo at Stanley Park Zoo, that one day when a group of people came to stare at the peacock, he was gone. The keeper told them he had died. Didn't he keep any of the bird's lovely feathers? the keeper was asked. Might they have one or two? The keeper shook his head. "All the glint went off 'em," he said, "when his heart broke."[207]

This writing style perfected by Carr, conveying pathos without sentimentality, proves that the artist was well aware of the degradation suffered by captive wild animals put on public display. Yet, as she told us in this same collection of stories, she herself was responsible for consigning to those conditions a wild animal whom she had taken into her domestic life when she realized, too late, that she could not realistically look after him.

He was a turkey vulture she called Uncle Tom, whom she had adopted from the wild during her time working in Vancouver during 1912–13. Carr stated in her story that she named the vulture "because of his resemblance to the picture in *Uncle Tom's Cabin*."[208] Harriet Beecher Stowe referred to vultures in the introduction of her novel as creatures who, like humans, "have the love of their offspring strong within them," underscoring the gross iniquity of separating enslaved families; Carr appears to have equated her black-feathered vulture's appearance with that of Tom in the novel, an insensitivity considered acceptable by many of her contemporaries.[209]

Tom had been brought to the mainland with a group of Sechelt men, who had taken him from his mother's nest on Texada, the largest island in the Salish Sea. Carr happened to be in Sechelt, where she met the band members and was shown the vulture chick. He was hungry and fading fast. Carr fed him clams she had dug up specially for him; then, pulling out fifty cents, she bought him from the villagers and then brought him back to her Granville Street studio. As Tom grew stronger and larger, he accompanied Carr on camping trips with her dogs and other birds. "He followed my every footstep," she wrote. "I was the only mother he had known." She also took Tom with her to meet her sisters in Victoria, where they made her keep him in a calf pen and to her frustration "could not accept [him] into the family circle," for reasons obvious to us though not to Carr.[210]

Carr does not say why she thought it was reasonable to keep a vulture, with a wingspan of roughly two metres, in a confined urban space, but her studio was lengthy and Tom got some exercise racing down the polished floor to get the meat Carr bought him from the butcher. She did, however, understand that she was responsible for what we now call "imprinting" Tom, and that he could never be released into the wild. There were likely comments from neighbours, aware of the bird's presence and his "queer, wild beast smell" (which sounded like something her sisters would say years later when Woo entered Carr's life). Carr realized there was no recourse but to offer Tom to the Stanley Park Zoo and cross her fingers that her decision was the right one. To her apparent surprise, he was accepted as a "curiosity" (in 1908, shortly after the new Monkey House had been completed).[211] Carr often visited Tom there in his cage. On these occasions, she told us, he pressed himself against the bars to "rejoice over me." He presumably wanted to be with the only human he had ever bonded with.[212]

By contrast, Carr's account of the unhappy end of her green parrot, Jane, no wild thing but a fully domesticated pet, leaves as bitter a taste as Tom's brief biography.

Jane was so domesticated she had learned from Carr certain English phrases. And she croaked a wobbly-voiced rendition of "God Save the King," which led Carr's neighbours at Granville Street to assume she boarded a demented old lady fond of singing the only tune she knew.[213] Jane had been with Carr for some time, and like the other animals, had been taken on sketching trips and the journeys back to Victoria, where she came to live when Carr moved into Hill House. This happy coexistence seemed to change with the coming of Woo. After a life together of some fifteen years, Jane began to act out in increasingly violent bids for attention. Extremely social, parrots require more attention, on average, than a dog. And it is telling that Jane's last episode with Carr, the one that brought her to a fateful decision, came while the latter was tending to a sick dog in her kennels. Having lost her long-time mate, the easy-going cockatoo, Sally, Jane may have been in emotional distress, a factor most bird fanciers would recognize. Today, a vet would prescribe a regimen of therapy, perhaps a protocol of medication for a bird in such a state. However, Carr's response to the behavioural oddities of an elderly parrot who had spent nearly all her life with her was to sell her.

When a woman answered the advertisement Car placed in a Victoria paper, Carr told her she was selling Jane because she was "wicked." So into this stranger's hands went Jane, and then out again, as Carr later discovered. Carr was told Jane had fallen in love with the woman's son, but when the young man went away to join the Navy, Jane became depressed and combative. So the woman, who similarly concluded that Jane was wicked, sold her on to a poultryman. When Carr, strangely eager to know what had happened to the bird she had given up so easily, caught up with the man and asked him about Jane, he told her he had found her a "malignant varmint," and so sold her to an individual who then left Victoria. That was where the trail went cold. They were discussing this when the woman Carr had sold Jane to came by chance into the poultry shop, and a joke was shared among the three that a carcass she was examining was in fact Jane. "The three of us doubled over laughing," wrote Carr. It's not Emily Carr's finest moment, and it says something about her that is not part of the genial, animal-adoring stereotype known to most people today. How could she profess to respect and love animals, and let this happen to Jane, a companion of many years, captured in "family portraits" and Carr's own sketches? How was this letting nature take its course? Did she really believe, as she had assured Carol Pearson, that the animals she gave up in this manner were still safe in the heart of God?[214]

But for me, the most troubling of all of Carr's sometimes matter-of-fact accounts of how she rendered life or death decisions for her animal family is one involving Woo. We may well ponder, in Carr's written accounts of Woo, why she could write, "What Woo learned about spanking she had not learned from me,"[215] citing the bullying of the elder monkeys toward Woo in Lucy Cowie's pet shop. After all, Edythe Hembroff-Schleicher casually referred to witnessing Carr punishing Woo with the flat of her hand, the way Carr might have administered punishment to a dog or cat she felt needed correction. It is well known that Carr's stories about her animals are a mix of fact and fiction, to be sorted through with care; but whether in her own memoir Hembroff-Schleicher was sharing a fiction rather than fact is another matter. Whatever the quality of her recollection of events from decades earlier, Hembroff-Schleicher's memory of Carr spanking Woo is not likely to have been invented simply because spanking was accepted as perfectly normal, buried in a narrative that instead focuses on Carr's irritability around other humans (though not with the dogs underfoot—for Carr, they were never in the way) and a severe modesty about the human body that Hembroff-Schleicher attributes to "her early prudish [Victorian] education." Per Hembroff-Schleicher, Woo had earned the beating for her behaviour.[216] So where Woo's welfare in the bigger picture is concerned—not daily life with Emily Carr but in terms of what Carr thought was appropriate for her—it is fair to wonder how seriously Carr took her responsibility toward the monkey, how carefully she considered her needs. The pinafores, teaching her to sew, enforcing discipline were all things a mother might use with a human child. There is plenty of evidence that Carr did see Woo in that light. How, then, to explain her misguided and, happily, unsuccessful effort to make Woo a mother herself?

Carr wrote of how deeply "maternal" she believed Woo to be, based entirely on the interest she showed when any of the dogs had puppies. When the mother left them in their bed, Woo would cuddle them until she returned. When a stray cat who lived in Carr's garden gave birth to kittens, said Carr, Woo could not keep away from the babies, stroking them even as the mother spit at and threatened her. Being drawn to infant animals need not have come necessarily from maternal instinct as much being based in the circumstances of what we may assume was Woo's own separation from her mother at a too early age, when she was captured for the exotic animal trade. But Carr was a woman of fixed ideas; Woo needed another Woo. On the strength of Woo's care for puppies and kittens, in the late

1920s Carr took the ferry to Vancouver, leaving Woo and the other animals with her sister Lizzie. Her object was to discuss with the keeper of the Stanley Park Zoo's Monkey House what he thought of her idea of bringing Woo over to be bred with a male macaque at the zoo, so she could become pregnant and have a baby monkey of her own to care for.

Knowing what we do of Woo's fear of other monkeys, the mind fairly reels to think of how she might have reacted to being placed in a cage with a male, let alone how she would cope, or not, with the process of procreation. One way a male macaque prepares a female for mating is to groom her, which presupposes the two are in proximity for some time before the actual mating takes place. Did Carr really believe Woo could be introduced to these conditions, with her known fear of other monkeys (Mitsey excluded), and be pliant enough for the breeding process to carry through to its conclusion? And if Woo had survived that part of the experience emotionally as well as physically, and given birth, what then? It is likely that Woo was taken from her own mother too young. Would she have known how to mother an infant herself? Biologists agree that a monkey who is brought up away from her mother and all that her mother would naturally teach her will in her turn be less able to mother her own children. Having been imprinted by Carr, a rivalry might have been set up wherein Woo might have expected Carr to do the raising of the baby.[217] In any case, if a baby of Woo's lived, how would Carr manage two monkeys, when one, chained and caged and disciplined, prone to poisoning herself by eating paint and throwing tantrums for attention, was more than she could handle?

Luckily for Woo, the keeper of the Monkey House advised against the plan. He warned Carr not to think of breeding Woo, as in his experience both a captive mother and her baby had a high risk of death from the act. This was apparently enough to convince Carr to drop the idea. And back in Victoria, Lizzie, enraged as usual by Woo's exploits while in her care, at least had the wisdom to concur with the keeper's verdict, no doubt because the last thing she wanted to see in her sister's household was another monkey.[218]

In the end, Carr was almost too wild herself to be sentimental, perhaps too wild to be as kind as was called for. "I tried to be plain, straight, simple and Indian," she wrote in 1937.[219] I think animals she saw as her spiritual brethren; their ways, which she observed without judgement, were as much a part of her personal drama as they were her heart—perhaps more so. As such, however, her animal family became very like the inhabitants in zoos, or those quieter versions of wild animals prepared for eternity by the taxidermists who were so busy during the Victorian age. They were objectified, made symbols of control the human did not have over any other part of her life, recipients of affections that could not be trusted to other human beings, even as barricades to the threats of such affection. Writing of her animal family, Carr said, "I couldn't imagine a world without the love and the interest of them. They put up with you when nobody else will." But when she no longer had time or energy for them, they were sent away, as if by a mother bird giving her nest a spring cleaning.[220] Carr leveraged a place outside the realm of judgement for herself, as if keeping to the high road absolved her of any guilt for what might happen to an animal who she, in the guise of an "Indian" woman whom she felt she was, managed to discard without tears.

Through sheer fluke, it seemed to us both, I found myself walking down a leaf-strewn Vancouver street in misty October 2017 with one of my heroes, the British conservationist Ian Redmond.

How had it happened, we both laughed, after being Facebook friends for several years, he in the UK and I in Canada, that he should be in town for the Forest Stewardship Council's 2017 General Assembly and, on his last afternoon, notice that I had posted a welcome on his page (six days late), realized his hotel and my residence were a five-minute walk apart, and suggested we meet for a cup of tea? And here we were.

Why is Ian among my heroes? Like his colleagues Dr. Jane Goodall and Virginia McKenna of the Born Free Foundation, for which he serves as senior wildlife consultant, Ian keeps to a tireless schedule, one that would defeat someone half his age, to educate humankind in the critical importance of preserving Earth's remaining wild creatures—not as zoo specimens but as fellow caretakers of the shrinking garden that is our planet, the only home we, animals and humans, will ever have. Because we need each other, more than most humans know.

Ian had worked with Dian Fossey in Africa—indeed, the killing by poachers of one of her most famous study subjects, the silverback gorilla Digit, served as a turning point in Ian's career path as a conservationist. He founded Ape Alliance, takes part in the Species Survival Network Primate Working Group, is vice-chair of the UK Rhino Group, has participated in over fifty documentaries about mountain gorillas and risked his life to infiltrate poaching rings.[221]

Ian had taken part in the 2017 Forest Stewardship Council General Assembly in Vancouver to try, again, to push through a motion to include humane practices toward wildlife as part of the body's overall goal of best practices in forest management. In the week he had been in town, he had not had time to visit Stanley Park, an irony we both noted. I suggested we might pass an hour walking through part of our urban forest before his flight home, and that a particular piece of ground in Stanley Park might be of especial interest to him—the Rose Garden, where the Monkey House once stood, where Woo had briefly lived. His warm, bearded face lit up, and off we went, my partner, Rudi, and our dog, Freddie, beside, behind or before us as Freddie's curious nose dictated.

With so much of the world's wildlife in peril, and the weight of that peril on the back of this mild-mannered man strolling beside me, I hesitated to use our brief time together to talk about a pet macaque who had died almost eighty years earlier. But the story of Woo poured out of me and, I found, into open ears and a welcoming heart.

I told Ian all I knew. Her capture in Java, the voyage across the Pacific and being offered for sale in Lucy Cowie's pet shop in Victoria. Her upbringing among the appurtenances of Emily Carr's household, sharing in the traumas and the triumphs of her life. Her removal from that household, the nailing of the crate, the sail across to Vancouver that bitter January and a new life begun in a cage in Stanley Park Zoo. The ladies who brought her treats each Sunday. The unknowable but painfully plausible heartache she must have suffered in her cage. And the end.

My voice cracked with emotion and I stopped talking. Ian, who was himself silent, taking in everything I told him, then said, "I'm reminded of a story that is gaining attention now in Gloucestershire, where I live," he told me. "Do you know about John Daniel, the gorilla of Uley?"

Accounts vary regarding how the infant gorilla who came to be called John Daniel ended up for sale in the expensive London department store Derry & Toms in 1918. According to one version, John's parents were shot by German officers in Gabon; another claims the men were French. He was likely not even a year old when captured. Near Christmas, as the world was beginning to try to heal from the Great War, Major Rupert Penny of the Royal Air Force paid three hundred pounds (roughly the equivalent of twenty-eight thousand Canadian dollars in 2018) for the gorilla, who for a time lived with Major Penny's young sons, wearing clothes, using dishes and utensils to eat with and playing with the boys in their home in Regent's Park. Through the cold winter, John learned to prod the fire to keep it going. The following year, Major Penny turned John over to his sister, Alyce Cunningham, who lived in a country house in Gloucestershire near the village of Uley. Miss Cunningham soon became the mother figure John had lost in Africa. She taught John to make his bed (he had his own room in her house), and he used the toilet and helped wash up dishes as if he'd been doing so all his life. At thirty-two pounds, the gorilla was the perfect size for the children of Uley, who brought him along on their adventures. John got into adventures of another sort too, when he discovered the village pub, where he was given cider (he was allowed to have port and sherry at home). At Miss Cunningham's parties, John Daniel was as well-bred as any of the human guests, showing he knew how to use a napkin and fold it once he had finished his meal.[222]

"A country house, or any house, is not the place for a gorilla," Ian told me. "But here's the thing. John Daniel flourished in Miss Cunningham's care. Something about how she lived with the gorilla, how she looked after him, something in the life of the village that loved him, seemed good for him, in the way his original life in the wild would have been good for him—better for him, of course, had he always lived there." This is, he added, still an area of contention in wildlife preservation, as one wing of conservation will push for a pure return to the wild at all costs, the life of the animal in the balance, while the other may caution a softer adjustment to what may be a wild environment barely remembered—for some animals kept as pets from babyhood, an environment of which they know nothing. These are concepts that can set up small-scale civil wars among conservationists, and it is a battle that is made the more contentious because both sides are right. But these were not concepts most people entertained at the time John lived with Miss Cunningham in the country house at Uley. As it happened, biology itself determined his fate. As John grew into his third year, he reached over two hundred pounds. His size and strength, and perhaps the occasional episode that frightened Miss Cunningham, led her to accept an offer to purchase John and take him to a place where he and others could be safe. An American bought him, claiming he would take John to live in a sanctuary in warm and sunny Florida. But what happened was the polar opposite. When John disembarked from the ship that carried him across the Atlantic, "wearing a natty sailor suit with gay ribbon trimmings," in March 1921, he was given straight into the hands of Ringling Brothers and Barnum and Bailey Circus, who arranged to display him in Madison Square Garden in a viewing cage that included a barred room with door where John had a bed to sleep in, but none of the privacy he had known with Miss Cunningham. By early April, John had retreated permanently to this bed, "paying no attention to the many people who tried to attract his attention by calls and peanut throwing." He closed the door, wrapped himself in a blanket, and soon became seriously ill with pneumonia. The head of the circus at least had the consideration to cable Alyce Cunningham, reporting John's illness and offering to pay her passage if she would come to see him straightaway. Horrified at the turn of events, Miss Cunningham did so, but a week before her ship docked in New York Harbor, John Daniel died. John Ringling himself was heard to claim that if he thought it would have saved John, he would have set him free "in a jungle." Yet that would have been as cruel as what had brought the young gorilla to a concrete jungle in the first place. John Daniel, mourned Alyce Cunningham, had had "the run of my house like a child, and did not know what it was like to be in real captivity." He remains captive even in death. His body was given to the American Museum of Natural History, which saw fit to have him stuffed and placed on display in October 1921. He's still there.[223]

"The people of the village are trying to get him back," Ian told me. "It's a sad story."

It was, and I saw how Woo's own life had put him in mind of it. Suddenly, as we spoke of John Daniel here among the dripping pines and cedars of misty Stanley Park, Woo seemed very close, less than real, more than ghost.

We climbed the slight rise leading up to the Rose Garden, which still lifted to grey skies a few gaudy blooms on skinny stems. On roughly that spot, had we hopped on H.G. Wells's time machine, pulled its lever and watched the date spin back to 1937–38, we would have found ourselves standing in some portion of the Monkey House, its humid air filled with screeches of primates and squawks of birds. As if really silenced by this din, we had nothing more to say—the taxidermied corpse of John Daniel in his glass coffin in

New York City, the spirit of Woo and indeed of all the animals who had once looked out at humans like us from behind bars, rendered words meaningless.

I glanced at my phone, conscious that Ian had a flight to catch that afternoon and fearing I had caused him a mad rush to the airport by using up all his brief time. But time was on our side, I was relieved to see. Then I noticed something else while scanning my phone. It was a new painting posted on the Facebook page of Pockets Warhol, a capuchin monkey and former pet since infancy who now lives in a primate sanctuary in Ontario.

Since 2010, when Pockets was first introduced to paint and canvas, he has produced hundreds of works. His paintings, collected by several celebrities involved with animal welfare causes, are priced up to four hundred dollars each, and have not only made Pockets one of the top-selling animal artists in the world, but helped support the programs of the sanctuary where he lives. Titled *Blue on Blue* by a sanctuary volunteer who oversees Pockets's care, this newly posted painting is a work of abstract shapes on a white canvas, in what has become Pockets's style—something like a cross between the stylized spontaneity of Jackson Pollock, with its marriage of colour, the force of gravity and the artist's keen sense of when to intervene in the process of creation, and the complex fibrillating rhythms of Wassily Kandinsky, which seem to bob and chirp like exotic birds in a jungle forest. And its colours, I couldn't help but notice, echoed a portion of the sky over our heads, where an odd streak of surprised blue revealed itself through a brooding cloud ceiling.

"Have you ever heard of Pockets?" I asked Ian. He listened as I told him what I knew of the monkey's story. Like Woo, Pockets was brought up in a house in British Columbia by a human female who became the only "mother" he'd known. When this woman, like Carr, found herself in later years unable to care for Pockets as he required, she placed him in the Ontario sanctuary. "Now he is living the life Woo should have lived," I said. "Not in a zoo among primates strange to him, but in a place of safety, where he can be among humans, the only primates he has ever known. Above all, where he can be safe, and loved."

We were quiet again, watching Freddie's dark Pomeranian fluff dart suddenly across the grass as far as his leash would allow toward one of Stanley Park's equally fluffy black squirrels, who sat nonchalantly chewing a nut. A survivor of a puppy mill, those breeding facilities where dogs are kept in caged, often filthy conditions, their health and welfare of less concern than the selling of their litters, my dog still has a fear of other dogs years after his rescue. Woo and Pockets were no more comfortable with other monkeys than Freddie is with other canines. It's humans they feel most comfortable with, though it could be said they had no more reason to trust humans than these animals they feared. I mentioned as much to Ian. He has, as I have said, a warm smile. Yet in its warmth is the sadness of an embattled compassion, of knowing the uphill climb to a world of kindness, for an eradication of deadly exploitation of our animal cousins, may never reach a plateau where the heart can at least catch its breath. But then he said, "Why don't you meet him, this artist?" And that's when I realized that while I still did not know how the fates had managed to bring us together for this extraordinary hour, on hearing his words I knew why, and what I had to do, if I was ever to come close to understanding the phenomenon that was Woo and her effect on the human beings around her—the human beings of Story Book Farm, whom I'd read made it their number one object to respect the individual dignity of a human-imprinted primate as much as they cared for its welfare. Human beings who would never allow that contract to lapse, no matter the judgments of those who could not or would not understand. And I was about to find out.

CHAPTER 10

Pockets Warhol

In December 2012, two years after Pockets found a place to call home, a baby Japanese snow macaque, clad in a shearling coat and diaper, was found wandering with fearful eyes outside an IKEA store in North York, Ontario. The IKEA Monkey, as he came to be known, whose actual name is Darwin, was clearly in a place where he did not belong. Aged between four and six months, at a time when he should still have been with his mother, he was captured by Toronto Animal Services and was transferred to Story Book Farm Primate Sanctuary in Sunderland, Ontario,[224] a haven Dr. Jane Goodall has warmly endorsed.[225] "For so many reasons it is wrong and cruel to have a monkey as a pet," said Daina Liepa, a volunteer at Story Book Farm. "We try to provide a home for them that is better than what they had in the past. There are no shearling coats and no nappies here."[226]

Located about an hour and a half drive northeast from Toronto, Story Book Farm is home to a number of rescued primates—nineteen at current count, from macaques to baboons to lemurs and capuchins and spider monkeys—from across the nation who are slowly reacquiring that knowledge of which human ownership deprived them: how to be a monkey. It was to this isolated spot that I found myself, one chilly weekend at the end of November 2017, driving my rental car from bustling Toronto, hoping to find answers, and hoping to find Woo.

I don't need much convincing that the greatest tragedy of a wild animal's life is for it to be taken from its natural setting, raised among human beings, and then ultimately failed through one means or another by that human setting. And there is a similar tragedy suffered by many domesticated animals, the dogs and cats and birds and rats to whom people pledge to bring comfort and security for the brief space of their life span, only to relocate, acquire a significant other with allergies or to experience an unforeseen breakdown for a variety of reasons, out of which the animal too often pays the highest price of all.

The life stories—as best they can be known—of Story Book Farm's residents, outlined on the sanctuary's website, give a snapshot of what can happen when a monkey gets caught up in the sticky web of human affairs.

Information I was able to find was sparse and chilling. Six of these primates started out or ended up in zoos, from the roadside variety to private menageries. Two of the lemurs came from a pet store, the very last place you'd want to see endangered animals like these. A squirrel monkey, Rudy, had been discovered, gravely ill, in a storage locker, where he and other exotic animals had been abandoned by a breeder. A gentle spider monkey called Mr. Jenkins went from being somebody's pet to being tried out in lucrative film work, then was dumped in a petting zoo when he failed to deliver on expectations. Five macaques, Boo, Gerdie, Cedric, Cody and Pugsley, were used in laboratory experiments; the latter three (who arrived after my visit) made history in 2018 as the first lab primates whose freedom was signed off on by the Canadian government, in co-operation with the lab where the monkeys had lived. Julien, a Japanese macaque, was housed sitting on a mound of his own excrement in all weather at a roadside menagerie in Ontario; he escaped and was on the loose for three weeks till recaptured, during which his companion, a female who had escaped with him, was killed. He had an obsession with self-mutilation, which included biting himself when stared at by human onlookers. One of the two capuchins at the Farm, black-tufted Cheeko, had come from a hard life in a garden centre greenhouse near Toronto, as can be seen in his atrophied tail muscles, worn teeth (most of them recently removed), broken finger and almost but not quite broken spirit.

Among these shattered but healing residents, twenty-five-year-old Pockets is the miracle baby.

Loved from day one, like Woo, Pockets had spent years in a comfortable house in British Columbia. He had a television to watch, companion animals (dogs and a guinea pig) he enjoyed and who enjoyed him and a human "mother" to look after him. When, after a dozen years, Pockets's guardian (whose name I am keeping confidential for this narrative) found her life pushing her in a direction that made caring for him difficult, she did not give him up to a zoo or a lab. After researching wild animal sanctuaries across Canada, she found Story Book Farm, brought Pockets there and spent days helping to acclimate him to his new home.

Pockets was why I had come two thousand miles and a country drive to the Farm, to meet this monkey who had so much in common with Woo except that his life as captive monkey had a happy ending. All that seemed a clear enough plan as I neared the finish of this book's journey.

However, my arrival at the sanctuary, with its charming red brick farmhouse at the top of a curving drive in the hilly farmland of Brock Township, was fraught with some unforeseen last-minute jitters. The last time I had been in the presence of caged animals was an afternoon in the summer of 1995 when a cousin visiting me in Portland, Oregon, asked to be taken to the Oregon Zoo. My experience of such places has always been a composite of thrill to see wild creatures at close range and sadness to witness their captivity.

This mixed impression began with my first (and last) visit to a circus, when I was about five years old. I had watched with the other children and parents as elephants suddenly entered a spotlit ring, shambling like old men in baggy pants, seniors being hustled faster than was agreeable to age or dignity. Even the baby elephant at the end seemed elderly, uncertain, blinking in the bright light. Their mountainous bulk, which most elephants prefer coated in mud after a river swim, was draped in the shimmering satin caparisons of clowns, against which their grey hide seemed elemental, dinosaurian, out of place under the big top. Yet they paraded so smoothly, trunk to tail, apparently oblivious to the noise, lights, sequins, rolling a red ball around, standing upright, dancing at the direction of the man with a stern smile. One would have thought they were having as much fun as the spectators, were it not for the dispiriting impression that they were working off a sentence with no expiry, the conditions of which mandated service with a smile. The elephants' eyes were hard to read, pressed deep into fringes of long lashes; yet one of them did look at me, just as it passed by. In that instant, there rose between me and her an alternate reality that screened out everything around us. Looking into that golden eye, I inhabited with her a piece of forest stillness sliced out of time. I could hear wild elephants' deliberate yet delicate footfalls crackling in the underbrush against the rainbow chirps of exotic birds, the silver symphony of cicadas, the silences that lay like calm valleys between each stentorious chorus of trumpeting … and then the baby, who had lost its grip on an adult's tail, ambled across the circus ring frantically trying to catch up, and the peaceful spell broke into hot lights and laughter. There would be no forest for these elephants, not even in fantasy.

Years later, that golden eye would haunt me in another wild captive face.

When I took my cousin to a zoo, so many years later as an adult, I did so concealing at first how uncomfortable I was. We walked through the exhibits—the bears and birds and tigers—and I watched as creatures still imbued with the yearning for privacy that all wild things desire, obsessively circled or bowed or fidgeted under the gaze and chatter of adults and children cluttering their enclosures' edges. But when we came to the monkey cage, I no longer had dominion over my own emotions. It started with the squealing of the children, scattered everywhere, pressed against the bars. I recognized the same look in the eyes of the capuchins who sat tensely on branches and rocks that I'd seen at the circus in the gaze of an elephant. It's a look remarkably human, actually. It is frustration, it is anxiety, both of which were easy to understand in creatures attempting to eat their midday meal under the onslaught of human curiosity. They sat with dark fingers pressing food to rapidly chewing mouths, eyes glittering blindly toward the noise and activity of the children. Between the two groups, there was no doubt in my mind which was the better behaved, but that isn't what drove me away. It was the monkeys' consciousness of their situation. Obviously I cannot prove that they were aware of the coldness of their cement box, of the irony of young *Homo sapiens* screaming at quiet, gentle primates. I cannot prove, any more than I can with the circus elephant and memories of his rightful jungle, that these capuchins were dreaming of lost worlds they may actually never have known. But in the eyes of one of the monkeys, which turned to meet mine, not with pleading but with puzzlement that did not flicker as it bolted its dinner, I saw the jungle dreams in my circus elephant's sad golden eye. Sometimes, as I came to see, it isn't merely the captivity that is so degrading and harmful. It's how this captivity prompts humans to act (sometimes very badly indeed) when they experience it—to treat the captive animal as some sort of living trophy.

When he volunteered at Fauna Foundation in Quebec, author Andrew Westoll—whose award-winning book, *The Chimps of Fauna Sanctuary,* I brought along with me on my trip to see Pockets—was confronted with a broad array of the psychological damage inflicted on apes whose lives are spent as laboratory specimens for biomedical research. Fauna's residents had been knocked out with dart guns a dozen times a month so they could be operated on or injected with human disease agents in a bid to find cures (in failed experiments, many of which fulfill the adage about repeatedly doing the same thing and expecting a different result) for purely human afflictions. On top of being physically abused in this way, these chimps who never saw the sky or felt grass eventually developed heartbreaking mental illnesses that, like the diseases tried out on them in hope of discovering a cure, proved indelible. Westoll wrote, "Every chimpanzee in here is struggling to overcome some level of psychological disturbance."[227] Fauna Sanctuary, he added, was not a "crazy house," but in truth that is what it could be called, strictly speaking, though unlike many places worthy of that epithet, Fauna tries its best to correct what damage it can. As I learned, some of Story Book Farm's residents, traumatized by their histories, are also still marked by what they've been through. As I stepped out of my car at the top of the drive, I wondered what I would see in the enclosures here, and whether I could handle it for the two days I planned to stay on site.

It was a kindly human who put me at ease.

Charmaine Quinn met me and gave me my first tour of the sanctuary. A deeply empathic Torontonian who is so at home in the countryside she can give directions citing the colours of barn roofs and the patterns of cows along a given route (and no wonder: she spends months each year not just here but helping orphaned primates in the jungles of Borneo and Central America), Charmaine volunteers for numerous animal welfare causes in Canada and abroad and is a veteran of all things Story Book Farm. Since 2010, Charmaine has been Pockets's muse, as well as his caregiver, studio assistant and surrogate mother. Her muse duties involve dribbling child-safe pigments on small squares of canvas, then sitting with Pockets while he paints his world-famous pictures. After he has finished, Charmaine gives his works evocative titles and signs them for the artist.

Pockets is Charmaine's special buddy, but she knows the stories and the secrets of all the rescued primates housed at the Farm, and as we crunched over a dusting of snow to the entrance and into the kitchen of the barn, she told me about some of them.

Gerdie and Boo, the rhesus macaques, were a case in point. They survived lives of lab experimentation before being retired to the Farm. Whatever they endured the pair could not tell us. But their physical scars were matched by many more nobody can see, whose symptoms lay deep and arose with sudden terrors no one could predict.

They looked the same but were quite different. Gerdie had the resigned calm of having accepted her fate, the stunned uncertainty of a prisoner handed a reprieve, which seemed to veil her wary eye. Boo looked not so much confused as outraged, her gaze—which Charmaine cautioned me not to meet—both fearful and challenging. Shared experience, however, bound them both to similar memories and matching fears that neither could forget.

Both would be doing their thing, Charmaine explained—Gerdie grooming Boo, Boo carrying her tattered stuffed toy about the enclosure—only to be set off by some trigger that sometimes could be predicted, other times not. It happened on my second day at the Farm. We were preparing the residents' meals at a large metal table in the kitchen, listening to Bing Crosby dreaming of a white Christmas, when a volunteer opened a stepladder that had been standing for some time against a door joist, in full view of Boo and Gerdie, so she could hang Christmas decorations on nails above. As soon as the ladder opened, however, both monkeys went berserk.

Unless you have experienced it, the fear expressed by a primate pushed to its limits, the frenzy of terrified hoots, grunts, screams, cannot be imagined, let alone described. It's the desperate shriek of a mother who has lost her child in a tragic accident. You cannot hear it without closing your eyes, trying not to think, just letting it happen and hoping there is a way to eventually bring peace to a tortured soul. For the moment, we all stood frozen as screaming blotted out the Christmas tunes wafting softly through.

"We have to be careful of triggers," Kim Meehan, a zookeeper with the Toronto Zoo who has volunteered her expertise at the Farm for several years, told me as Gerdie and Boo quieted down and gradually returned to their previous activity. "We don't always know what they are or why they are triggers. We just have to watch for what they are and try to be careful." What a mournful realization amid the holiday cheer, the warmth and safety of this place, that even here, demons can intrude.

But just as past terrors can erupt without warning, however, so can evidence of healing appear without anyone, even professionals like Kim, being prepared for its revelation. This was evident when I went with her to meet the larger primates: Darwin (always playing outside, as to be expected of a healthy young male macaque); the baboons, handsome Pierre and gentle Sweet Pea (among the first to comfort Darwin on his arrival at the Farm); and the Japanese macaques, Julien and Lexy.

After we'd given everyone their dinner of fruit, vegetables, nuts and tofu, Kim stood alongside Julien's enclosure and held out an arm. She's a woman of quiet composure, with emotions that run deep. I sat behind her on a stool, resisting the urge to look at Julien, who I could tell was often looking at me. Kim spoke softly to the macaque. Would he like to groom her? Just this once? Her gesture had been met with indifference so often over the past several years that there was no reason to assume it would not continue to be the case, especially with me nearby to distract Julien. But Kim persisted. And then we both watched in amazement as Julien stretched from the enclosure grille a tentative brown hand, palm down and fingers relaxed. It is the one part of a monkey that physically most resembles ours; the gesture of reaching and responding to that reach is especially moving when it happens between us and our closest relatives. Occasionally looking up at Kim, Julien then touched her forearm with his fingers and began to busily pick away at its surface, lifting bits of skin, real and imagined, to his pink lips. Kim's back was turned to me, but I saw it tremble, heard a subtle but sharp intake of breath and watched as tears sprang down her otherwise impassive features.

When Julien, finished with his work, ended the grooming session a few minutes later to finish his dinner, Kim turned to me and whispered, tearful but smiling, thrilled almost to breathlessness, "It has taken so long, and now, suddenly, this *trust*. It is a great breakthrough, because it means we can build on this for his happiness. I'm so happy you could see how this works." So was I. It is one thing to try to judge from appearances how well the Farm's work was delivering on its credo, "We are a place of healing and recovery from trauma," quite another to see it happening before one's eyes, and quite wonderful to see its effect on a human being whose life and expertise are devoted to that end.

I had been following the photos and videos of Pockets on the Farm's Facebook page and Twitter feed for several years, but to meet him in person was a special delight because it is obvious this is a monkey who has always been loved and who has never known fear.

Nicknamed Pockets Warhol by Charmaine (who saw pop artist Andy Warhol's distinctive wrinkled pink face in his), he has become the famous capuchin artist of Story Book Farm, whose abstract works have been collected by a range of animal welfare activists—from Dr. Jane Goodall to comedian Ricky Gervais—and by private citizens of similar bent who love his work and, by supporting it, significantly help fund Story Book Farm. And Pockets serves as an educator as well as an artist. Charmaine proudly told me that he and his painting *Queen* would be featured in the 2018 second edition of National Geographic's *Wonderful World 1*, a series for young people introducing them to planet Earth in all its wild and wonderful variety.

Of all the monkeys at the sanctuary, Pockets seems not to need to think about it first before leaping up to say hello, even to a stranger. He has no roadside zoos, no lab experiments, no rejection in his past. He has been allowed to develop as normally as a wild animal can do in a setting of purely human domesticity. The demons that pursue the others are unknown to him; even his enclosure, which for wire grille and wooden posts and sawdust-strewn cement floor is no different from the other residents' areas, seems to emanate a light that cannot be accounted for by the presence of the window which, on the day I visited him, gave out on a silver-lit and snowy afternoon. Pockets glows still brighter.

Pockets and Woo, separated by over half a century between her death in 1938 and his birth in 1992, were not a perfect parallel by any means—I knew that. Unlike Woo, shipped to a zoo after Carr's hospitalization, Pockets had been rehomed by a guardian who had not done so forced by age or illness but because she realized that as circumstances changed, she could no longer care for him as he deserved, and that her responsibility toward him continued full force up to and after finding him the perfect new home to land in. Differences aside, Pockets and Woo were monkeys who spent all their lives with humans and were thus specially vulnerable to problems associated with that relationship. Pockets was what Woo could have been, had she had the soft landing that was his happy fate—proof that animals can make us better humans, if we only just let them.

Pockets's transfer from guardian to sanctuary had no shadows about it. He had one human mother looking after him and now has several, above all the devoted Charmaine, whose connection with "Pocks" is quiet, deep and also sweetly playful. One morning, when I was sitting by myself, squirrel monkey Rudy energetically vaulting over the branches in his enclosure, George crooning for love and Mr. Jenkins lounging like a mellow Buddha, I had a glimpse of what a human can mean to a monkey and vice versa.

When Pockets paints, only Charmaine is allowed to be with him, and while she occasionally videos this activity, it is clear from the strict solitude accorded the little artist, as he delights in the colours that flower across his canvases, that Charmaine sees these as sacred moments, not to be intruded on, proper to a creative soul. (I know, because Charmaine disappeared the Sunday I was at the Farm, returning after less than an hour with a painting by Pockets, her eyes shining with the fresh thrill of a process she has overseen hundreds of times. She named the painting, based on the colours Carr used in her 1945 portrait of her monkey muse, *Woo's Apples*.)

On this occasion, however, I was privileged to have a front row seat to the continued flowering of their friendship. I watched as Charmaine shut herself inside Pockets's enclosure, and after she spent a few moments tidying the space, setting his toys upright and shaking out his blankets and towels, I saw her come to him, murmuring without words, and hold him, clean him and caress him, while he responded with something between coos and a sort of breathless purr, his up-tilted hazel eyes fixed on the face of the gentle woman touching him.

Remembering this scene later on, charmed, moved, angry, I was prompted to say to Kim, "If only Woo could have had this life. Not ladies bringing candy on Sundays to her cage at a zoo. Not kisses sent by proxy from Victoria. Not strangers and confusion and misery. This love and safety." And I went on like that for some time.

Kim is a no-nonsense person and has a guarded quality to her nature where humankind are concerned; the only time she softened, that I could see, was when she talked to the monkey residents. This easy manner of communicating with monkeys lives alongside a definite air of authority, that of a complete professional with facts at her fingertips and a disciplined approach to caring for Story Book Farm's residents. "Don't get them all excited," she chided me one morning as I approached Pockets's enclosure to give him his breakfast, at the same time reinforcing his gleeful gambols with my clumsy middle-aged male mugging. Kim had earlier seen me playing maniacally with Pockets as he pushed his toys, which include a series of dinosaurs and a snorting pig, through the interstices of his enclosure at me. She had also witnessed how my interaction just afterward with another volunteer in Pockets's presence had caused the monkey to cry out at me in jealous frustration, his fists tight and eyes flashing angrily—not unlike the outraged Woo when she feared having to share Ginger Pop with Lucy Cowie's monkey, Mitsey, or when she had to share Emily Carr with anybody, human or animal. I was told I should leave the barn to let Pockets cool off. "He doesn't want to share you," Charmaine had said, trying to smooth things over. But I understood, thanks to Kim, just how serious this was. These were living, feeling beings, whose emotions were not to be toyed with. She made me more aware of this than when I had arrived at the Farm, far more aware, and she reminded me of something else I needed to know.

As I finished my complaint about Woo's fate, Kim gave me that same look, the one your best teacher at school shot you when you tried to palm off a half-baked answer, though knowing better.

"Should we be judging Emily?" she asked me. "Don't you think she wanted love and safety for Woo?" she added.

These were heavy words; I let them sink in.

It goes without saying that what happened to Woo in January 1937 was unfortunate—we can all agree on that. I had spent the past two days going over the story again and again, almost obsessively, with Kim, Charmaine, Daina, Amy, Rachelle, Anita and Sarah, and we'd all had tears talking about it. Woo's amazing life with Carr. Woo's terrible separation from her. That year in Stanley Park Zoo. How Woo had died alone.

I realize Carr's options were few. After all, she was very ill—was told by doctors and reminded by her sister that she might die at any time. She was also poor and had few options when it came to finding the most appropriate homes for her animal family. She happened to know the keeper of the Monkey House, and when prompted, this ordinary fellow did what he could to help her. That was where Woo's story snarled for me. It is the way it was done, the way Woo was caged like a zoo exhibit, never to know Carr's touch again, always to be vulnerable to the prodding of strangers, the tossed cigarette butts and chewing gum of a careless public. I had read of the importance of social touching—how, without it, human orphans had a 30 to 40 percent mortality rate, even when fed and looked after properly in all other respects. During Woo's year at the zoo, Carr asked her Vancouver friends: "Please kiss Woo for me." But what was that kiss to Woo? I had witnessed at Story Book Farm what a long-awaited visit could mean to a monkey missing his human friend. One day a volunteer, who had not been to the Farm for a few days, entered the kitchen and prompted spider monkey George to make passionate whistles, hoots and cries at the very sight of her. Though like all the volunteers she had a lot of work to do—cleaning and sweeping and emptying and filling—she made sure to visit George, scratching him through the wire grille. Another volunteer for whom George opened his heart actually entered his enclosure to hug him. I saw how his lanky, dark form moulded limply to her embrace, like a grateful child; heard sounds like both sobs and laughter in his throat, like a child being comforted by his mother, and heard him cry again when she had to leave.

Was it like that for Woo? Can we bear to think so?

Again Kim asked, "But what about Emily?" And, as I realized, she was right.

Well and good for me to come to Story Book Farm to observe best practices, to meet monkeys who would never again be betrayed. Well and good for me to deplore the abuse many here had suffered at some human hands, to celebrate their healing at the hands of others. I had not thought much at all about the cost Emily Carr bore to lose Woo.

Overnight, her peaceable kingdom of animal family, the very foundation of her world as artist and woman, was scattered. Her life was to be rebuilt new, and indeed, Carr's fame rests on the next eight years of her life, on her way to becoming the cultural icon she is today. But in those first days home from St. Joseph's, surely her much-desired "Indian" fortitude, practised but never mastered and never hers to own to begin with, quaked after her return to the cottage on Beckley Street to the kitchen where Woo had lived, to her slack chain and collar, her empty cage. What was that homecoming like for the sick artist? We are only beginning to understand complicated grief, which exists for humans who have lost loved animal companions as for those who have lost human loved ones. Grief over loss of a loved one is normal. Most people work through it over time. Complicated grief is a different thing entirely. It can last for years, causing long-term health problems physical and mental, and is tied up with guilt and anger and helplessness. Though she gradually acquired a few dogs, a bird, a squirrel, surely there were nights in Beckley Street when Carr turned her thought, however reluctantly or painfully, to Woo, sitting somewhere miles away among the trees and strange monkeys of Stanley Park, and wondered. And wept. Yes—that, at the very least, and likely not for the last time. The very fact that Woo was on her mind when her own end came seems to confirm all of the above.

"Please think of Emily," Kim insisted, and I did. And it dawned on me that I had come all this way, from the rainforests of British Columbia to the snowy fields of northern Ontario, not just to meet Pockets, but to come to grips with Carr. She looked at me steadily out of the kind, honest faces of these women at Story Book Farm, whose compassion had room, alongside that for innocent betrayed animals, for those humans who did try their best and who must not be blamed if their best fell short of the ideal, not least because if those humans had failed, at least they had loved. Whose eyes asked me to summon not sympathy, nor pity, nor any particular emotion (that quality Carr tended to take with a grain of salt anyhow), but just to try to *understand*.

Later that evening, as I stood in the snow, looking at a pink and gold sunset recalling a Pockets Warhol masterpiece, I knew where I needed to go next.

EPILOGUE

Apple Tree

I had spent more time inside Emily Carr's apartment house in my imagination, reading her accounts of clashes with her tenants, adventures with her animals and the discoveries that made her the revered artist she is today, than I did actually going to see the property, which still stands in Victoria's James Bay neighbourhood, just down the slope from Beacon Hill Park.

I remember, years ago, driving past Hill House once or twice while en route to someplace else, slowing down, having a look and then moving on, thinking, "Well, it's nice it's still there." It wasn't, after all, the crown jewel in the city's Emily Carr treasury. That was the lovely yellow villa, now a museum, just around the corner from Hill House. Built by Richard Carr, the Emily Carr House's high-ceilinged rooms are silted up with the magic and mayhem of Emily's tragicomic childhood. I'd once been allowed to spend an hour alone in its parlour. I'd sat at the doily-draped upright piano, the wall above hung with framed prints of ladies in hoop skirts, and I played a Beethoven sonata with rusty technique, wondering whether Edith or Lizzie would have minded. (Or Carr herself: she loved good music, loathed what amateurs like me did with it.) I had also simply sat there and watched the play of shifting afternoon light across the precious clutter of Victorian decor. Woo had never been here, but the playful simian character of Emily's childhood self seemed to gambol about these gracious rooms, breaking nothing but coming close, much as Woo might have done.

Yet, just as had happened at Story Book Farm, where I went in search of a specific thing and found an answer I didn't know I was really looking for, in the process of searching for Woo I discovered that the Carr House and Hill House were two very different places, and while the same in some respects, were as different from each other as, in Emily Dickinson's words, an orchard from a dome. And in realizing that difference, I finally found Woo.

My visit to Hill House, accompanied by my partner, Rudi, and our dog, Freddie, started with a moment of silence in Ross Bay Cemetery, where Emily Carr and her family lie under the overarching rib vaults of old, sea-salted trees. It was one of those chill, bright Victoria spring mornings when sun slices down through sheets of rain, dry brief partings that made nonsense of an umbrella, only for skies to open and winds rise and make even more nonsense of it by turning the thing inside out.

Carr's grave lies within sight of the busy boulevard of Fairfield Road, with its close-packed detached houses and low-rise condo complexes. Close, too, seem the Carrs, all of them wedged into the small concrete-bordered plot, so tight a tomb to contain such a larger-than-life family. They rest there in intimate proximity that the open air seems to have promised would not be cumbersome and, having discovered the lie, can be imagined tossing in irritable restlessness.

It is easy to believe, though, that even in death Carr has other things on her mind—that, as in life, she looks past the bonds of mortal family to the wider embrace of Nature, which never constrained her as flesh and blood did. So when you approach her grave, you do so with the sense of interrupting Carr's communion with a handsome old Garry oak that stands a few yards from her feet. You notice the smallness, flatness, finality of the stone grave marker, which was put there in the 1960s, onto which, as in the family plot, a few words attempt to encapsulate the vastness of who Carr was: "Emily Carr, 1871–1945, Artist and author, lover of nature."[228] Arranged around the smooth rectangle, or jabbed into the space between its hard edges and the softly overgrown grasses, are paintbrushes, pencils, pens—the tools of Carr's trade. The morning of my visit, there were other gifts too: a pin featuring the Canadian flag; a rhinestone brooch, long and languid, like the type of jewel Carr's sisters might have worn at their high-necked collars on some rare day meriting a bit of extra sparkle. And then you notice the granite plinth beside the gravestone. On this piece of rock, which in its heft and roughness seems a match for any ancient Garry oak, are carved words that are as much prayer as epitaph:

> Dear Mother Earth! I think I have always specially belonged to you. I have loved from babyhood to roll upon you, to lie with my face pressed right down on to you in my sorrows. I love the look of you and the smell of you and the feel of you. When I die I should like to be in you uncoffined, unshrouded, the petals of flowers against my flesh and you covering me up.

You read this and you almost wish there were nothing here. No concrete border. No other Carrs jostling for space in that earthy embrace Carr's true mother meant for her alone. No historical cemetery full of worthies with their names on streets and in crumbling documents in archives, with whom Carr had nothing in common, whose lives are nowhere written upon the sky as Carr's is. She should have been buried in a field, like the one carpeted with white lilies where Carr had her last picnic with her maternal namesake. Someplace where nobody even knew where to find the grave, or even knew a grave was there, because Mother Earth had taken her daughter into her arms, and to interpose was to disrupt a supreme law of Nature.

And someone has remembered Woo. Propped against the granite plinth, below Carr's ringing encomium to Mother Earth, is a wooden plaque on which a monkey, carved in relief, clings to the thick stem of some tropical tree. Its worried expression makes it appear to be thinking, "Now that I'm up here, how do I get down?" I smiled, having felt that way myself often enough on my journey in search of Woo. Rudi, Freddie and I stood for a moment of silence, in which it seemed a monkey might descend, chattering, at any instant. Freddie certainly seemed to expect this, though perhaps it was just the cautious squirrels crouching in the trees overhead. Then we headed for the car and for Hill House.

As we stood out front on the Simcoe Street sidewalk waiting for the arrival of Hill House's owner, the cries of Beacon Hill Park peacocks tumbling down through the quiet morning. Peter Willis, the property's owner, pulled up in his truck. Like me, he had grey at his temples, and his smile showed me how delighted he was to be giving me a tour of the house, the history of which, I could see, still filled him with awe. Peter inherited the property from his mother and leased its units to tenants. As we shook hands, he told me regretfully that because the space that formerly housed Carr's studio was occupied, we couldn't visit it that day. This led us to converse about the many alterations made to the building, which took place almost from the beginning of Carr's ownership.

"Oh yes, many changes," Peter said, squinting against the morning light. He told me, for example, that there was no front entrance for the original building; there didn't need to be, as tenants each had their own front door—Carr wanted to make sure she did not have to meet them unannounced, and above all that each lived his or her life separately from each other, as she wanted to live hers separate from theirs. Over time, Peter said, windows were replaced or moved, and during Carr's lifetime she had walls put up or pulled down to ensure the most commodious results for renting extra space and making extra money.

Peter took Rudi, Freddie and me around the west side of the house, toward a little picket gate. I distinctly recalled the 1920s and 1930s photographs capturing Carr and her animals in the green-branched Eden behind Hill House. The bobtail sheepdogs. The birds. The cats. The griffons. Woo. Whether purchased or seized as the wild things to which Carr was inexorably attracted, they had found sanctuary here, much as our Freddie had been rescued from squalor and neglect a few years earlier and has a safe and loving life with us.

"I should really get back here with the mower," said Peter, grinning. "Her dogs are buried in the garden, you know," he told us in the glimmering gold-green light. "This is where she had their kennels also," Peter said. "Gone a long time ago." We looked through the multi-trunked cedar, past an empty fountain surrounded by shrubbery, and toward a stalwart old apple tree, standing almost in the centre of the garden, equidistant between Hill House and the fence beyond. I glanced at Freddie, wondering if he could sense the ghosts of a menagerie cavorting in the morning air, wishing he could tell me.

I asked Peter what had happened to the cherry tree, where Woo had sat shooing birds from the fruit. Peter told me the tree had been in bad shape and had to be taken down quite some time ago. "But look, the apple is still here," he added. Peter and I walked toward the old apple tree. I noticed the crazed akimbo angles of its branches, the thick grey hide of its bark. It bore both green and red fruit, he assured me. He was sure, he said, that the tree was here when Woo lived in Hill House.

I touched the bark, looked up through twisted branches beginning to flesh out with early spring leaf, where I saw a small iron ring that obviously was nailed into the bark many decades ago, high up near the crook of the tree. Studying the ring, I wondered whether it had ever tethered Woo. I noted something else too—something familiar in the tree's shape, colouring, something that I couldn't place or name. But time was too short for musings. I filed the impressions away for later.

"Let's go into the basement," Peter suggested, and we headed underground.

My grandparents—probably your grandparents too—had such a daylight cellar as Hill House has. My grandmother kept her trousseau trunks down there, each filled with old fans, lace, embroidery, packets of scentless sachet and boxes of unused and now useless Edwardian hat-wire. Along with these trunks there were crates full of odds and ends on shelves above a dirt floor, old ice skates hanging from hooks above. A hint of the tomb's dusty finality over all. And impenetrable mystery.

Like my grandparents' cellar, Hill House's is accessed via an exterior door. Like theirs, this one was gloomy, with light just managing a dim egress through small, square windows. It was just as low of ceiling as my grandparents' basement. The cement floor, apparently laid later, afforded us better footing, though the increased height made the floor joists above seem impossible to avoid, endangering the head of the visitor unwise enough to forget to stoop.

Off to one side, there was a shelf, plain wood painted a brownish colour, original to the house. "Emily would have stored things in there," Peter told me, showing me an interior filled with a variety of the sort of items one keeps in a cabinet in the cellar—gardening gloves and clippers, some tools and some bits of wood. On the shelf's walls was the occasional fleck of smeared bright green or yellow pigment, like bits of forest light and foliage, from long ago—had Carr stored her paints here? The dark space invited us to keep guessing.

We moved around a corner into a broad but low and strangely cave-like space, where Carr's coal furnace used to stand, and where Woo once slept. The east-facing windows where she had sat on sunny winters over ninety years ago, charming passersby with her scowl, were covered in sheet plastic, dimming the glow of morning.

From the depths to the heights: Peter then sent us up the two-storey back stairs while he ran round to the front of the house, promising to meet us at the top. While we waited, I tried to imagine what the view had been like from this second-storey landing in Carr's lifetime. The verdigrised copper domes of the Parliament buildings bubbled up past distant treetops; beyond them rose the white eyries of the Olympic range in Washington state. My eye fell to the garden again, and to the apple tree, which now seemed even more self-possessed, planting its old feet sturdily in young grass.

A narrow door, filled with prim glass panes, opened to Peter's smiling face, and in I went to join him. We stood in a very high upstairs hall with doors opening off it (one into the former studio). Peter pointed upward and asked if I could see through a narrow window above. I followed his arm and yes, I did see a little window, and through it the outlines of a Haida-style eagle, strong black brushstrokes flowing across the underside of the eaves.

Peter set up the rickety aluminum triangle of a stepladder, which did not reach quite high enough, it seemed to me. He told me it was easy. (He's also far more athletic than I am.)

He ascended first, removed the glass pane covering the aperture and was soon inside the attic with practised speed. My climb was far less graceful, but as I struggled through the aperture fourteen feet in the air, I reflected on the parable of the camel passing through the eye of a needle, and that getting to heaven was not meant to be an easy journey.

And it was heaven indeed. Raising myself from the dusty floorboards of the attic, I stood slightly bent over in what amounted to a storage space between the ceiling of the room below and the peak of the roof above. But as my vision cleared and Peter switched a bare light bulb to life, I settled into what the area really was. It reminded me of certain old chapels I've been to—the more holy for being empty. Carr's attic felt like a cave of meditation, made sacred not by some ascetic's solo prayers but by the fact it had sheltered a busy creator, continues to shelter examples of her painting all the more rare for existing outside the confined control of a museum, all the more personal because these artworks were initially meant for her eyes alone.

I remember reading in Carol Pearson's memoir how the author, as a child, would bed down in here, and how Carr told her that the eagles would protect her during the night. Over our heads they continued to fly, bands of dark red frogs at their clawed feet. And this reminded me of another sacred space I once visited, a longhouse in Alaska. There, too, a small door, a difficult fit for a broad-beamed middle-aged man, proved worth the struggle by the hard-won benediction of reaching and standing silent in its gorgeous, unspeakably sacred interior.

That Carr herself had spent much time here was obvious, and that art was not always on her mind was obvious too. Peter showed me a list of Carr's dogs, pencilled on a wall. Carr's tortuous handwriting flowed down the water-stained and cracked expanse of matchboard, listing dogs with names like Pearl, Lollipop, Spider and Sugar Plum, their ages and increasing weight, from 1922 to 1923. The latter year made me think of Woo, who had joined these dogs around that time.

Peter also had Woo on his mind. "You can see how Emily tried to Woo-proof this space," he told me, pointing to bits of chicken wire nailed over various openings and to a board set up at the end of the crawl space between this attic and the one on the east side of the house. His children have found scratch marks on the wood, presumably from Woo's nails as she vaulted from space to space. The mind's eye, enchanted by shadows and these outspread eagles overhead, easily imagined and even saw the scamper of a dark figure from the eagle chapel.

And then, that was it. We looked at the locked door of Carr's former studio, turned and went. My brief tour was already over. But, in truth, my thoughts had already departed Hill House. I descended the two flights of squeaky stairs to the garden, where the prescient, amused silence of Nature seemed to await me.

I went again to the apple tree, and that was when I saw more clearly through the foggy impression I'd had earlier. The crooked-armed branches and the green apples of this tree are echoed in Carr's final painting of Woo from winter 1945.

I pulled up the painting on my phone and realized what I was remembering was more the ghostly spirit of a tree than a real one. The jutting branches of the painting are less natural, random growth and more like dark arms terminating in grasping hands that deliberately reach for Woo. They could be all the fingers of strangers coming at her in her cage in Stanley Park, all the claws of monkeys she was thrown together with on her infant sail across the Pacific. All the wordless things she meant to Carr, that she means to us.

Yet, she doesn't care. She's safe. She's free both from the restraints of life with her human mother and from whatever laws Nature might try to impose on her, in that timeless, lawless netherworld that is art, and that is death.

Some, looking at this painting, see a sinister expression on Woo's pointed face. I study the gleaming apple held firmly in her slender fingers, and I see something else: the triumph of a spirit released from bondage.

Perhaps this, one of Carr's last paintings, was her way of telling the world, in the best language she knew, that of volume, form and colour, that she had come to terms with her part in Woo's beginning and her end, just as she realized that Woo had played a significant role in Carr's own end and beginning. It is not a memory of sorrow or regret, but of celebration.

I had with me a book. Lilian M. Russell's *My Monkey Friends* was published in London in 1938. Mine, with its chipped dust jacket, is the second edition. I'd found the small volume in a used book shop in Sidney, a town north of Victoria. *My Monkey Friends* tells the story of Mrs. Russell's rescue of and adventures with various orphaned monkeys brought to her, or who came to her, during her years in Africa as a young girl and, later, as assistant to the famous medical missionary Dr. Albert Schweitzer. I brought the book with me to Hill House because I had recently discovered it connects me to Carr and, especially, to Woo, in a strikingly real way.

At Christmas 1948, not long before Mrs. Russell died, she inscribed this copy to someone she knew well enough to add "with love." The book's owner was none other than Lucy Cowie, former proprietor of the Bird and Pet Shop on Government Street in Victoria. In the post-war years, Mrs. Cowie was living on Burrard Street in Vancouver, in one of the quaint semi-detached two-storey bungalows that have largely disappeared from the downtown's modern glass and steel core. Like the Monkey House in Stanley Park, the building where the Cowie bungalow stood is a short walk from where I once lived in the West End. Ghosts, the spectres left behind by these buildings seem to say, are more real than you can ever know, and closer than you think.

That Lucy Cowie owned this book in and of itself suggests that she had had a change of heart where her practice of selling monkeys was concerned. Mrs. Russell pulls no punches in that regard, pointing out that she only came in contact with the monkeys she described, and took them into her life, because they would otherwise have died as orphans (not unlike Allen Hirsch's Benjamin in 1990s Venezuela), and would never encourage anyone to purchase a monkey. Not only would such a person be supporting "a horrible form of trade" in wild animals, she wrote, but few humans are capable of keeping up with, and keeping happy, a monkey in a domestic setting. The book's final chapter is full of advice to those who share their lives with a monkey. "Respect his personality," she adjured. "Give them the understanding love they demand. [They will] make you realize that even the love of a monkey is a manifestation of the all-embracing love of God."[229]

I read part of this last chapter to Peter as we stood under the apple tree. I had earlier shaken him more than I intended by telling him that Woo had not spent her last days with Carr, as he (and many) assumed, but in a cage at the Stanley Park Zoo. "She's right," he said quietly, when I finished. "Nobody should keep a wild animal." I nodded, saying, "I'm pretty sure the fact that Lucy owned this book, and knew its author, means that she must have seen the error of her ways," and we both paused a moment to think about what that realization might have felt like to a woman who had made her living off the sale of monkeys like Woo, who had a chance to make it right before she died. I hoped she did.

Did Lucy Cowie wonder how many stolen lives she put a price on? Peter smiled sadly at my question. "I'm pretty sure," he said, "that Emily must've come to that realization too."

I smiled at that thought, and I knew he was right.

I pulled up Carr's wild final portrait of Woo again and held it up beside the tree. And it seemed to me, touching the harsh crust of bark, that seven years after the monkey's death at Stanley Park Zoo, and many more than that since Woo had lived at Hill House and gambolled in these branches, Carr's heart, hurt but not broken, and infinitely wiser, had indeed wandered back to this garden and to this tree, to the memory of the moody simian muse who had helped her become the artist and person she was meant to be, and had captured her again, this time to let her go.

ENDNOTES

Prologue

1 For map, see David Loughnan, *My Visit to Stanley Park: A Photographic and Descriptive Story of Stanley Park, British Columbia*, Vancouver: Uneeda Printers Limited, 1950: 36–37.
2 Pete McMartin, "A flamingo killer in the family leads to threatening phone calls and tears," *Vancouver Sun*, May 21, 1992.
3 Sean Kheraj, *Inventing Stanley Park: An Environmental History*, Vancouver: UBC Press, 2013: 201–2.
4 Emily Carr, *The Heart of a Peacock*, Vancouver: Douglas & McIntyre, 2005: 183.
5 Carol Pearson, *Emily Carr as I Knew Her*, Victoria: Touchwood Editions, 2016: 62.
6 Carr, *Peacock*, 242.
7 Pearson, Emily Carr, 120.
8 Terry O'Reilly, "Mail order monkeys & other crazy comic book ads," CBC Radio, February 15, 2018. According to O'Reilly, between 1968–1972, more than 173,000 monkeys were shipped from South America to the United States.
9 Phyllis Marie Jensen, in discussion with the author, February 2017.
10 Emily Carr and Ira Dilworth, *Corresponding Influence: Selected Letters of Emily Carr and Ira Dilworth*, ed. Linda Morra, Toronto: University of Toronto Press, 2006: 28.
11 J. Allen Boone, *Kinship with All Life*, New York: Harper & Brothers, 1954: 7.

Chapter 1

12 Gerard Manley Hopkins, *The Later Poetic Manuscripts of Gerard Manley Hopkins in Facsimile*, ed. Normal H. MacKenzie, New York and London: Garland Publishing, 1991: 129.
13 "Our Emily: Emily Carr Statue," heroines.ca. Major funders for the Carr statue were, besides the province of British Columbia and the federal government of Canada, Shaw Communications of Calgary, Frank and Elizabeth Garnett, the Audain Foundation for the Visual Arts, actress Clarice Evans of Calgary (the only woman listed on the statue's plaque), Enbridge Inc. of Calgary, the N. Murray Edwards Charitable Foundation of Calgary, the W. Garfield Weston Foundation in Toronto and the John C. Kerr Family Foundation of Vancouver.

The Fairmont Empress Hotel donated the piece of ground on which the statue stands, and the *Times Colonist* newspaper was an active in-kind partner. I thank writer Virginia Watson-Rouslin, prominent early supporter of the Carr statue, for her recollections.

14 Emily Carr, *Opposite Contraries: The Unknown Journals of Emily Carr and Other Writings*, ed. Susan Crean, Vancouver: Douglas & McIntyre, 2003: 83.

Chapter 2

15 Carr, *Peacock*, 174.

16 Virginia Woolf, *Flush: A Biography*. New York: Harcourt, Brace and Company, 1938: 48.

17 "Puppies Attract Victoria Kiddies," *Daily Colonist*, August 3, 1923: 9.

18 Lucy Alexander married Alfred Cowie, a native of Manitoba, in Glasgow on October 10, 1919: marriage record, District of Pollokshields in the Burgh of Glasgow: 210.

19 "Puppies Attract Victoria Kiddies": 9.

20 Scotland Census, Parish: Ardoch; ED: 1; Page: 4; Line: 13; Roll: CSSCT1901_115.

21 Canada Voters Lists shows Alfred Cowie, telephone installer, living in Vancouver: Voters Lists, Federal Elections, 1935–1980, R1003-6-3-E (RG113-B), Library and Archives Canada, Ottawa.

22 Lilian M. Russell [Mrs. Charles E.B. Russell], *My Monkey Friends*, London: Adam & Charles Black, 1948: 123. Lucy Cowie's copy is in possession of the author.

23 "Puppies Attract Victoria Kiddies": 9.

24 Hannah Velten, *Beastly London: A History of Animals in the City*, London: Reaktion Books, 2013: 166.

25 Isak Dinesen [Karen Blixen], *Out of Africa* & *Shadows on the Grass*, New York: Vintage Books, 1989: 287–89.

26 Viktor Reinhardt, "Artificial Weaning of Old World Monkeys: Benefits and Costs," *Journal of Applied Animal Welfare Science* 5, no. 2 (2002): 149–54. Dr. Reinhardt added in an email to me on September 24, 2018: "By the way, what's true for monkeys is true for cattle. We studied semi-wild cattle in Kenya and found that the calves form affectionate bonds with their mothers that last for many years, leading to the establishment of tight family bonds. When calves are prematurely weaned, the associated distress reduces (not enhances!) the mother's reproductive performance." The maternal bond, known to be vital to life itself in humans, must finally be seen, based on solid research, as playing just as vital a role in the lives of animal mothers and their children.

27 Carl D. Soulsbury, Graziella Iossa, Sarah Kennell and Stephen Harris, "The Welfare and Suitability of Primates Kept as Pets," *Journal of Applied Animal Welfare Science* 12, no. 1: 10.

28 Carr, *Peacock*, 175.

29 Emily Carr, *This and That: The Lost Stories of Emily Carr*, ed. Ann-Lee Switzer, Victoria: Touchwood Editions, 2007: 167–69.

30 John Adams, Victoria historian and writer, in discussion with the author, March 8, 2017.

31 Carr, *This and That*, 167–69.

32 Desmond Morris, *Monkey*, London: Reaktion Books, 2013: 46.

33 Margaret Wade Labarge, *A Baronial Household of the Thirteenth Century*, Toronto: Macmillan, 1965: 184.

34 Emily Carr, *The Book of Small* in *The Complete Writings of Emily Carr*, Vancouver: Douglas & McIntyre, 1993: 95.

35 John Adams, in discussion with the author, March 8, 2017.

36 Carr, *Book of Small*, 94.

37 Carr, *Book of Small*, 144.

38 Carr, *Opposite Contraries*, 83.

39 Carr, *This and That*, 169. Carr is known to have ventured as far east as Whitechapel via omnibus. For additional reading, see Maria Tippett, *Emily Carr: A Biography*, Toronto: House of Anansi Press, 1977: 41. Opened in 1828, the London Zoo, in addition to becoming a repository of animals for scientific study, also served as the new home for wild animals formerly kept in the Tower of London, where there had been a menagerie since medieval times. In 1905, there were three areas in London Zoo where primates were displayed: an enclosure for "Outdoor Monkeys," a long "Monkey House" structure parallel to Terrace Walk, and roughly forming the third point to a triangle, the "Apes' House."

40 Velten, *Beastly London*, 166.

41 Carr, *This and That*, 169.

42 Carr, *Peacock*, 176.

43 Edythe Hembroff-Schleicher, *M.E.: A Portrayal of Emily Carr*. Vancouver: Clarke, Irwin Co., 1969: 49.

44 Emily Carr, *The House of All Sorts*, in *The Complete Writings of Emily Carr*. Vancouver: Douglas & McIntyre, 1993: 238.

45 Ross King, *Defiant Spirits: The Modernist Revolution of the Group of Seven*. Vancouver: Douglas & McIntyre, 2010: 333.

46 Emily Carr, *Hundreds and Thousands*, in *The Complete Writings of Emily Carr*. Vancouver: Douglas & McIntyre, 1993: 676. Could Pearl have been the young woman named Mollie Robinson, age twenty-one in 1921, who is listed on the census of that year living as Carr's boarder at 646 Simcoe Street, occupation "student" at Sprott Shaw College (a business school)? Mollie is not shown as paying rent, unlike Carr's tenants listed above her on the census form. Perhaps, as Carr was short of money, Mollie was working for her as maid in exchange for board and keep. A search through the 1921 census for Victoria for women with the given name Pearl turns up either children or married women, none of them in domestic service. Source: RG 31; Folder Number: 20; Census Place: Ward 5, Victoria (City), British Columbia; Page Number: 11.

47 Carr, *Peacock*, 176.
48 Ibid., 177.
49 Carr, *House of All Sorts*, 206.
50 Carr, *Peacock*, 177.
51 Ibid., 178.
52 Ibid.
53 Ibid., 179.
54 Ibid.
55 Emily Carr, *Emily Carr and Her Dogs: Flirt, Punk & Loo*. Vancouver: Douglas & McIntyre, 1997: 31.
56 Carr, *Peacock*, 179.
57 Carr, *Opposite Contraries*, 131.

Chapter 3

58 Emily Carr, *Pause: A Sketchbook*, in *The Complete Writings of Emily Carr*, Vancouver: Douglas & McIntyre, 1993: 621.
59 Carr, *Book of Small*, 104.
60 Carr, *Peacock*, 23.
61 Carr, *Book of Small*, 113.
62 Ibid.
63 Carr, *This and That*, 168–69.
64 Carr, *Peacock*, 186.
65 Russell, *My Monkey Friends*, 14–15.
66 Pearson, *Emily Carr*, 58.
67 Carr, *Peacock*, 181.
68 Pearson, *Emily Carr*, 57.
69 Carr, *Peacock*, 181.
70 Pearson, *Emily Carr*, 120.
71 Carr, *Peacock*, 181–82.
72 Ibid., 180.
73 Ibid., 187.
74 Carr, *Emily Carr and Her Dogs*, 37.
75 Author and Peter Willis, visit to Simcoe Street April 14, 2017.
76 Carr, *Hundreds and Thousands*, 775.
77 Soulsbury et al., "Primates Kept as Pets," 11.
78 Carr, *Peacock*, 185–86.
79 Ibid., 180–81.
80 Ibid., 195.
81 Ibid., 184.
82 Pearson, *Emily Carr*, 10.
83 Richard Sewall, *The Life of Emily Dickinson*. Cambridge, MA: Harvard University Press, 1994: Vol. 1, 58.
84 Carr, *Peacock*, 188.

85 Ibid., 189.
86 Ibid.
87 Ibid., 191.
88 Ibid.
89 Ibid., 190.
90 Ibid., 192.
91 Florence Nightingale, *Notes on Nursing: What It Is and What It Is Not*, London: Harrison, 1860: 147.
92 Carr, *Peacock*, 192.

Chapter 4

93 Sharyn Rohlfsen Udall, *Carr, O'Keeffe, Kahlo: Places of Their Own*, New Haven, CT: Yale University Press, 2001: 174.
94 Carr, *Opposite Contraries*, 130.
95 Dyllan Furness, "Do Animals Appreciate Art?" *Creators*, June 30, 2017.
96 Carr, *Opposite Contraries*, 63.
97 Ibid., 130.
98 Emily Carr, *An Address by Emily Carr*. With an introduction by Ira Dilworth. Toronto: Oxford University Press, 1955: 10.
99 Carr, *Opposite Contraries*, 114.
100 Carr, *This and That*, 171.
101 Carr, *Opposite Contraries*, 86.
102 Furness, "Do Animals Appreciate Art?"
103 Ibid.
104 Ibid.
105 Carr, *Opposite Contraries*, 124.

Chapter 5

106 Edythe Hembroff-Schleicher, *Emily Carr: The Untold Story*, Saanichton, BC: Hancock House, 1978: 14.
107 Phyllis Marie Jensen, *Artist Emily Carr and the Spirit of the Land: A Jungian Portrait*, London: Routledge, 2015: 193.
108 Pearson, *Emily Carr*, 27.
109 Ibid., 28.
110 Allen Hirsch, in discussion with the author, July 5, 2017. Hirsch and Benjamin's relationship was the subject of a documentary, *Long Live Benjamin*, which won the 2018 Emmy Award for Outstanding New Approaches: Arts, Lifestyle and Culture.
111 Carr, *Peacock*, 211.
112 Allen Hirsch, in discussion with the author, July 5, 2017.
113 Carr, *Peacock*, 193–94.
114 Ibid.
115 Ibid., 226–27.

116 Charles Darwin, *The Expression of the Emotions in Man and Animals, New York: D. Appleton & Company, 1886:* 132.

117 Carr, *Peacock*, 226.

118 Ibid., 226–27.

119 Ibid.

120 Merlin Donald, *Origins of the Modern Mind: Three Stages in the Evolution of Culture and Cognition*, Cambridge, MA: Harvard University Press, 1993: 146.

121 Ewen Callaway, *Nature*, January 9, 2015: www.nature.com/news/monkeys-seem-to-recognize-their-reflections-1.16692

122 Peter Wohlleben, *The Inner Life of Animals: Love, Grief and Compassion—Surprising Observations of a Hidden World*. Vancouver: Greystone Books, 2017: 108–10.

123 Steven M. Wise, *Rattling the Cage: Toward Legal Rights for Animals*. Cambridge: Perseus Books, 2000: 268.

124 Carr, *Peacock*, 226–27.

125 Ibid., 198.

126 Ibid., 199.

127 John Gray, *Straw Dogs: Thoughts on Humans and Other Animals*. London: Granta Books, 2003: 110.

Chapter 6

128 Hembroff-Schleicher, *M.E.*, 32.

129 Emily Brontë, "Stanzas," *Poems by Currer, Ellis, and Acton Bell*. Urbana, Illinois: Project Gutenberg: www.gutenberg.org/files/1019/1019-h/1019-h.htm.

130 Jensen, *Artist Emily Carr*, 66.

131 Pearson, *Emily Carr*, 18–19.

132 CBC, "The Life and Times of Emily Carr," broadcast October 4, 1996.

133 Pearson, *Emily Carr*, 40–41.

134 Carr, *This and That*, 141–42.

135 Carr, *Peacock*, 186–87.

136 Ibid.

137 Ibid., 186.

138 BBC, *Life of Mammals*, Episode 10, February 5, 2003.

139 "Gorilla Reunion: Damian Aspinall's Extraordinary Gorilla Encounter on Gorilla School" (published on YouTube April 21, 2010 by AquaVita Films).

140 "Wounda's Journey: Jane Goodall releases chimpanzee into forest" (published on YouTube December 17, 2013 by Jane Goodall Institute of Canada).

141 Pearson, *Emily Carr*, 37.

142 Hembroff-Schleicher, *M.E.*, 31.

143 Pearson, *Emily Carr*, 63–64. Woo's interest in magazines recalls Dr. Jane Goodall's account of a home-raised chimpanzee called Lucy, who without prompting would choose a magazine from the living-room table and flip through its pages with interest or lack thereof depending on what she saw on

each page. After Lucy, who knew enough American Sign Language to describe to Goodall what she liked in the magazine, closed it, she told Goodall in ASL that the magazine belonged to her, Lucy. Jane Goodall, *Through a Window: My Thirty Years with the Chimpanzees of Gombe*, Boston: Houghton Mifflin, 1990: 13.

144 Pearson, *Emily Carr*, 59.
145 Ibid., 80–81. Lilian Russell noted that Kawa did the same. See *My Monkey Friends*, 17.
146 Richard Natoli-Rombach, in discussion with the author, June 28, 2017.
147 Carr, *Peacock*, 213.
148 Morris, *Monkey*, 70.
149 Ibid., 187.
150 Pearson, *Emily Carr*, 10.
151 Tippett, *Emily Carr*, 192–94.
152 Carr, *Address*, 13.
153 Carr, *Hundreds and Thousands*, 685.
154 Ibid., 692.
155 Carr, *Opposite Contraries*, 77.
156 Carr, *Hundreds and Thousands*, 694.
157 Pearson, *Emily Carr*, 67.
158 Carr, *Opposite Contraries*, 74.
159 Carr, *Hundreds and Thousands*, 740.

Chapter 7

160 Jensen, *Artist Emily Carr*, 194.
161 Carr, *Hundreds and Thousands*, 813–17.
162 Ibid., 823.
163 "The Famous Artist Next Door" Parts 1 and 2, *Islander Magazine*: http://victoriahistory.ca/blog/2010/08/the-famous-artist-next-door and http://victoriahistory.ca/blog/2010/08/the-famous-artist-next-door-part-two.
164 Ibid.
165 Carr, *Hundreds and Thousands*, 818.
166 Ibid., 832.
167 Ibid., 829–30.
168 Ibid., 842.
169 Ibid., 851.
170 Ibid., 850–51.
171 Ibid., 851–52. I myself have witnessed or been involved in two different scenarios relating to what can happen to the beloved pets of an elderly guardian who becomes too ill or infirm to care for them, or who dies and leaves them behind. When my grandparents died, their small dogs, a pug and a spaniel, elderly and set in their ways, came to live with my parents. For a long time, they were very confused; having been doted on for years in my grandparents' home,

they were unhappy with the pets that were already there in their sudden new place of residence. And, sadly, they never really adjusted during their final few years of life. In another instance, when a family member was diagnosed with dementia and had to be moved to a setting that would not allow him to keep three cats, I was given the unenviable task of finding a home for one of them. This was a sad problem that was happily solved, I am relieved to say, because I canvassed the board of the local animal shelter and called on friends of friends to help. The cat spent very little time at the shelter, going straight into the arms of her loving new family. It does not always end this way—indeed, it often ends the way it did with Woo, because who has the time or the contacts, especially among the ill and elderly? That someone like Carr, who may have believed she was working against a short timeline of life, was expected to find homes for all her animal family—specifically for the most difficult-to-place member of that family—is also not so greatly different to today's outcomes where the elderly are concerned. And given the circumstances, it is not surprising that she could find nobody who wanted Woo.

172 Doreen Walker, ed. *Dear Nan: Letters of Emily Carr, Nan Cheney, and Humphrey Toms*. Vancouver: UBC Press, 1990: 59. The name of Carr's female griffon, Vanathe, resembles the Hindu name Vanathi, which means "of the forest"—perhaps suggested by Carr's friend the Hindu Christian lecturer Mr. Singh?

173 Carr, *Peacock*, 242.

174 Despite a diligent search in the Park Board archives for the name of a keeper of the Monkey House from this period, I have been unable to identify him.

175 It was to Willie that Carr gave her first portrait of Woo, now in the collections of the Royal BC Museum in Victoria.

176 Carr, *Opposite Contraries*, 136.

177 Carr, *Opposite Contraries*, 138.

178 Carr, *Peacock*, 242.

179 Heini Hediger, *Wild Animals in Captivity: An Outline of the Biology of Zoological Gardens*. New York: Dover Publications, 1964: 27–28.

180 Carr, *Hundreds and Thousands*, 730.

Chapter 8

181 Major J.S. Matthews, *Early Vancouver, Volume 3*. Vancouver: City of Vancouver, 2011: 285.

182 Ibid.

183 Richard M. Steele, *The Stanley Park Explorer*. Vancouver: Whitecap Books, 1985: 116, 129.

184 Alan Mikhail, *The Animal in Ottoman Egypt*, New York: Oxford University Press, 2014: 168. As of this writing, the tomb of a lady believed to have been the grandmother of Qin Shi Huang, first emperor of China, has been discovered near the emperor's famous mausoleum in Shaanxi province. In the tomb of Lady Xia was a veritable zoo of wild animals—leopards, lynx, bears, cranes.

An ape skull found there belongs to a species of gibbon believed to have gone extinct largely through the type of capture and collecting that resulted in Lady Xia's private zoo of 2,200 years ago. See Gretchen Vogel, "Vanished ape found in ancient Chinese tomb, giving clues to its disappearance," *Science*, June 21, 2018.

185 Vancouver Park Board minutes, April 13, 1933.

186 Kheraj, *Inventing Stanley Park*, 136.

187 Historian Richard M. Steele poked fun at the SPCA in his history of Stanley Park, sending up the organization's efforts to improve the lives of the animals in the zoo as symptoms of the eccentricity many still believe inherent in the actions of animal welfare activists, by noting its concern for the animals during World War II should the park be bombed by enemy aircraft (the SPCA asked that the zookeeper be authorized to euthanize the animals in the event of such a catastrophe). He also unfortunately politicized the efforts of proto-NDP MLA Edward W. Winch of Burnaby for his work to guarantee the zoo's bears more adequate living space than what the zoo afforded them. Richard M. Steele, *The Stanley Park Explorer*, Vancouver: Whitecap Books, 1985: 117–118.

188 Book 9, Minutes, Park Board Commissioners, 1609, December 9, 1932. Ironically, there is today a fund benefiting the BCSPCA in James Fyfe-Smith's name.

189 Ibid. Along with researching the minutes, I searched the Park Board Annual Reports from 1936–39, and found nothing relevant to the Stanley Park Zoo Monkey House or, indeed, the zoo, with the exception of a reference to the buffalo enclosure. The Park Board Annual Reports are lists of expenditures and income; the zoo brought in nothing to speak of, and it appears repairs to its facilities were either not needed or were paid for through other means, or simply not carried out.

190 *Province*, March 27, 1928, 81.

191 *Vancouver Sun*, March 28, 1928.

192 *Province*, March 27, 1928, 81.

193 St. Paul's Anglican, Vancouver, BC, "Peace by to the whole community: The story of St Paul's in the West End"; "1603 Franklin Street," *Changing Vancouver: Then and Now Images*.

194 Fred Thirkell and Bob Scullion, *Frank Gowen's Vancouver: 1914–1931*, Victoria: Heritage House, 2003: 76, 80.

195 Kheraj, *Inventing Stanley Park*, 136.

196 Walker, *Dear Nan*, 59.

197 Hembroff-Schleicher, *M.E.*, 65.

198 Walker, *Dear Nan*, 72.

199 Walker, *Dear Nan*, 116–17. Had Woo lived another year, in May 1939 she and her fellow inmates of the Monkey House could have looked through their bars and watched King George VI and wife Queen Elizabeth walking up the pathway past the Rose Garden to a reception in their honour at the Stanley Park Pavilion, as noted in the 1939 Park Board Annual Report (dated January 18, 1940).

200 Carr, *Peacock*, 242.
201 University of Exeter, "Social ties help animals live longer," *Science Daily*, May 16, 2017.
202 Tippett, *Emily Carr*, 271–73. This painting of Woo, now in the collection of the National Gallery of Canada, is listed in that institution's catalogue as having been painted "circa 1932." However, as Tippett demonstrated in her Carr biography, Carr referred to putting the finishing touches to the painting in an undated note sent to Ira Dilworth in the year of her death. See Tippett, Chapter 13, n. 69.
203 Tippett, *Emily Carr*, 278.

Chapter 9

204 Tippett, *Emily Carr*, 222.
205 Pearson, *Emily Carr*, 62.
206 Carr, *Peacock*, 21.
207 Ibid., 35.
208 Ibid., 36.
209 Harriet Beecher Stowe, *Uncle Tom's Cabin*, London: John Cassell, 1852: Introduction, iv.
210 Carr, *Peacock*, 36.
211 CVA Park Board, Superintendent Report 11, p. 8.
212 Carr, *Peacock*, 37.
213 Ibid., 40.
214 Ibid., 45–46.
215 Ibid., 224.
216 Hembroff-Schleicher, *M.E.*, 32–33.
217 Janine M. Benyus, *The Secret Language of Animals: A Guide to Remarkable Behavior*. New York: Black Dog & Leventhal Publishers, 2014: 95.
218 Carr, *Peacock*, 202–3.
219 Carr, *Hundreds and Thousands*, 389.
220 Ibid., 208.
221 "Renowned conservationist Ian Redmond survives elephant charge": see bornfree.org.uk, June 27, 2016.
222 Jane Ridley, "UK villagers to NYC museum: Release our pet ape from your exhibit!" *New York Post*, February 18, 2017.
223 Ibid.

Chapter 10

224 Jacques Gallant, "Ikea Monkey's former owner gives up legal battle to get Darwin back," *Toronto Star*, February 28, 2014. In a related case, as of this writing, celebrity Justin Bieber is in the news again regarding Mally, a capuchin monkey seized from him in 2013 by authorities in Germany. According to the zoo where Mally lives, he is unable to communicate normally with other

capuchins. It is believed Bieber purchased Mally on the black market. See Tosten Burks, "German Zoo Says Justin Bieber's Illegal Monkey 'Still Has Issues,'" *Spin*, January 11, 2018.

225 Jane Goodall, jacket blurb for *Pockets Warhol's Art Collective* catalogue.

226 Katie Grant, "'Ikea Monkey' Darwin adapting to normal life two years after internet stardom," *The Independent*, January 29, 2016.

227 Andrew Westoll, *The Chimps of Fauna Sanctuary: A Canadian Story of Resilience and Recovery*. Toronto: HarperCollins, 2011: 19.

Epilogue

228 On my visit to Ross Bay Cemetery, as described in this book, I took my dog, Freddie, to Emily Carr's grave. He sat beside the marker, looking across all the graves into the distance, and was as well behaved as he is in every place we take him. To my surprise, while researching Carr's grave's history, I found that dogs are by law not permitted in Ross Bay Cemetery (Ross Bay Cemetery Bylaw No. 10-046, Part 7, 46 [1]). While I can see the practical reasons for this prohibition, I also wonder what Carr would think of being laid to rest in a place where dogs are not allowed to come and sit beside her grave. I don't know that a dogless afterlife is what Emily Carr had in mind. I do know she believed rules are made to be broken, and I imagine she would agree with my opinion on this particular case.

229 Russell, *My Monkey Friends*, 123, 127.

BIBLIOGRAPHY

Bekoff, Marc and Jessica Pierce. *The Animals' Agenda: Freedom, Compassion, and Coexistence in the Human Age*. Boston: Beacon Press, 2017.

Benyus, Janine M. *The Secret Language of Animals: A Guide to Remarkable Behavior*. New York: Black Dog & Leventhal Publishers, 2014.

Boone, J. Allen. *Kinship with All Life*. New York: Harper & Brothers, 1954.

Bradley, Laura. "Frida Kahlo's Monkeys, Dogs and Birds," *AnOther Magazine*, October 13, 2011: www.anothermag.com/design-living/1467/frida-kahlos-monkeys-dogs-birds.

Burks, Tosten. "German Zoo Says Justin Bieber's Illegal Monkey 'Still Has Issues,'" *Spin*, January 11, 2018: www.spin.com/2018/01/justin-bieber-monkey-still-has-issues.

Callaway, Ewen. "Monkeys seem to recognize their reflections," *Nature* , January 9, 2015: https://www.nature.com/news/monkeys-seem-to-recognize-their-reflections-1.16692.

Carr, Emily. *An Address by Emily Carr*. With an introduction by Ira Dilworth. Toronto: Oxford University Press, 1955.

———. *The Book of Small*. Vancouver: Douglas & McIntyre, 2004.

———. *Emily Carr and Her Dogs: Flirt, Punk & Loo*. Vancouver: Douglas & McIntyre, 1997.

———. *The Heart of a Peacock*. Vancouver: Douglas & McIntyre, 2005.

———. *The House of All Sorts*. Vancouver: Douglas & McIntyre, 2004.

———. *Opposite Contraries: The Unknown Journals of Emily Carr and Other Writings*, ed. Susan Crean. Vancouver: Douglas & McIntyre, 2003.

———. *Pause: A Sketchbook*. Vancouver: Douglas & McIntyre, 2007.

———. *This and That: The Lost Stories of Emily Carr*, ed. Ann-Lee Switzer. Victoria: Touchwood Editions, 2007.

Carr, Emily, and Ira Dilworth. *Corresponding Influence: Selected Letters of Emily Carr and Ira Dilworth*, ed. Linda Morra. Toronto: University of Toronto Press, 2006.

Darwin, Charles. *The Expression of Emotions in Man and Animals*. Chicago: University of Chicago Press, 1965.

DeSoto, Lewis. *Extraordinary Canadians: Emily Carr*. Toronto: Penguin Canada, 2008.

Dinesen, Isak [Karen Blixen]. *Out of Africa & Shadows on the Grass*. New York: Vintage Books, 1989.

Donald, Merlin. *Origins of the Modern Mind: Three Stages in the Evolution of Culture and Cognition*. Cambridge, MA: Harvard University Press, 1993.

Fagan, Brian. *The Intimate Bond: How Animals Shaped Human History*. London: Bloomsbury, 2015.

Furness, Dyllan. "Do Animals Appreciate Art?" *Creators*, June 30, 2017: https://creators.vice.com/en_us/article/d38zwz/animals-appreciate-art.

Gallant, Jacques. "Ikea Monkey's former owner gives up legal battle to get Darwin back," *Toronto Star*, February 28, 2014: www.thestar.com/news/gta/2014/02/28/darwin_the_ikea_monkeys_former_owner_loses_appeal_to_get_him_back.html.

Goodall, Jane. *Through a Window: My Thirty Years with the Chimpanzees of Gombe*. Boston: Houghton Mifflin, 1990.

Grant, Katie. "'Ikea Monkey' Darwin adapting to normal life two years after internet stardom," *The Independent*, January 29, 2016: www.independent.co.uk/news/weird-news/ikea-monkey-darwin-adapting-to-life-two-years-after-internet-stardom-a6842061.html.

Gray, John. *Straw Dogs: Thoughts on Humans and Other Animals*. London: Granta Books, 2003.

Green, Valerie. *Above Stairs: Social Life in Upper-Class Victoria 1843–1918*. Victoria: Touchwood Editions, 2011.

Hediger, Heini. *Wild Animals in Captivity: An Outline of the Biology of Zoological Gardens*. New York: Dover Publications, 1964.

Hembroff-Schleicher, Edythe. *Emily Carr: The Untold Story*. Saanichton, BC: Hancock House, 1978.

———. *M.E.: A Portrayal of Emily Carr*. Vancouver: Clarke, Irwin Co., 1969.

Hopkins, Gerard Manley. *The Later Poetic Manuscripts of Gerard Manley Hopkins in Facsimile*, ed. Norman H. MacKenzie. New York and London: Garland Publishing, 1991.

Jensen, Phyllis Marie. *Artist Emily Carr and the Spirit of the Land: A Jungian Portrait*. London: Routledge, 2015.

Kheraj, Sean. *Inventing Stanley Park: An Environmental History*. Vancouver: UBC Press, 2013.

King, Ross. *Defiant Spirits: The Modernist Revolution of the Group of Seven*. Vancouver: Douglas & McIntyre, 2010.

Labarge, Margaret Wade. *A Baronial Household of the Thirteenth Century*. Toronto: Macmillan, 1965.

Loughnan, David. *My Visit to Stanley Park: A Photographic and Descriptive Story of Stanley Park, British Columbia, Canada*. Vancouver: Uneeda Printers Limited, 1950.

Masson, Jeffrey Moussaieff. *Beasts: What Animals Can Teach Us About Human Nature*. London: Bloomsbury, 2014.

Matthews, Major J.S. *Early Vancouver, Volume 3*. Vancouver: City of Vancouver, 2011.

Mikhail, Alan. *The Animal in Ottoman Egypt*. New York: Oxford University Press, 2014.

Morris, Desmond. *Monkey*. London: Reaktion Books, 2013.

Nightingale, Florence. *Notes on Nursing: What It Is and What It Is Not*. London: Harrison, 1860.

O'Reilly, Terry. "Mail order monkeys & other crazy comic book ads," CBC Radio, February 15, 2018.

Pearson, Carol. *Emily Carr as I Knew Her*. Victoria: Touchwood Editions, 2016.

Reinhardt, Viktor. "Artificial Weaning of Old World Monkeys: Benefits and Costs," *Journal of Applied Animal Welfare Science* 5, no. 2 (2002): 149–54.

Roberts, Veronica. "A Close Look: Frida Kahlo's *Fulang-Chang and I*," *Inside/Out*, December 3, 2009: www.moma.org/explore/inside_out/2009/12/03/a-close-look-frida-kahlo-s-fulang-chang-and-i/.

Russell, Lilian M [Mrs. Charles E.B. Russell]. *My Monkey Friends*. London: Adam & Charles Black, 1948.

Sewall, Richard. *The Life of Emily Dickinson*. Cambridge, MA: Harvard University Press, 1994.

Soulsbury, Carl D., Graziella Iossa, Sarah Kennell and Stephen Harris. "The Welfare and Suitability of Primates Kept as Pets," *Journal of Applied Animal Welfare Science*, 12:1-20, Milton Park, UK: Taylor and Francis, 2009

Steele, Richard M. *The Stanley Park Explorer*. North Vancouver: Whitecap Books, 1985.

Stowe, Harriet Beecher. *Uncle Tom's Cabin*. New York: Penguin, 1981.

Taylor, Charles. *Six Journeys: A Canadian Pattern*. Toronto: House of Anansi Press, 1977.

Thirkell, Fred, and Bob Scullion. *Frank Gowen's Vancouver: 1914–1931*. Victoria: Heritage House, 2003.

Tippett, Maria. *Emily Carr: A Biography*. Toronto: House of Anansi Press, 1979.

Udall, Sharyn Rohlfsen. *Carr, O'Keeffe, Kahlo: Places of Their Own*. New Haven, CT: Yale University Press, 2001.

Velten, Hannah. *Beastly London: A History of Animals in the City*. London: Reaktion Books, 2013.

Walker, Doreen, ed. *Dear Nan: Letters of Emily Carr, Nan Cheney, and Humphrey Toms*. Vancouver: UBC Press, 1990.

Westoll, Andrew. *The Chimps of Fauna Sanctuary: A Canadian Story of Resilience and Recovery*. Toronto: HarperCollins, 2011.

Wise, Steven M. *Rattling the Cage: Toward Legal Rights for Animals*. Cambridge: Perseus Books, 2000.

Wohlleben, Peter. *The Inner Life of Animals: Love, Grief and Compassion—Surprising Observations of a Hidden World*. Vancouver: Greystone Books, 2017.

Woolf, Virginia. *Flush: A Biography*. New York: Harcourt, Brace and Company, 1938.

ACKNOWLEDGEMENTS

This journey into the life of Woo began over ten years ago. It was an idea that remained loyal to me even when I frequently brushed it away to make time for other book projects that took me far from the stage of Woo's charmed life. Yet in a significant way, this book created itself while I tagged along and tried to keep up—somewhat like spending time with a monkey. It stayed true through life changes, residential moves, musical chairs day-job adventures and more than one breaking and resetting of my life structure.

Two beings I love for many reasons, apart from the fact that they, too, stay true through storms, deserve all the gratitude I can give them, and then some—my partner, Rudi Klauser, and our dog, Freddie.

Without Rudi's encouragement and belief in me, I could not have pushed this years-in-the-making project through to completion. Without his love, I could not have summoned the courage to do so. And with Freddie sitting at my feet through research, writing and editing, the often painful process of bringing a book to birth was eased and the author's spirits raised immeasurably. I thank and love you both.

I owe thanks to others without whom this book could not have been.

It was to Jan Ross, curator of the Emily Carr House in Victoria, that I first confided my interest in writing a life of Woo. Sometimes years elapsed before I contacted her again, and each time, there she was, full of encouragement and advice. She helped me in tangible ways—connecting me with all the right people so I could visit the

House of All Sorts—and in intangible ways, simply by believing there was magic in the life of the monkey who shared fifteen glorious years with Emily Carr. Thank you, Jan.

Without the generosity of Peter Willis, owner of the House of All Sorts, in showing me all the places where Woo spent so many happy years, from its secret garden to its attic eyrie, I could not have rounded out a life story that I first approached from the place where it ended, the Rose Garden in Stanley Park. Thank you, Peter.

Deepest thanks to Jolene Cumming, founder of the Stanley Park History Group and the Stanley Park History Salon, and co-founder of the Herstory Café. The wealth of history she carries in her head matches the rich compassion in her heart, and the encouragement she has given me since I first contacted her, out of the blue, about a monkey who lived in Stanley Park eighty years ago, has educated, guided and inspired me. Thank you, Jolene.

I shared the manuscript of this book with Dr. Kathryn Bridge, former deputy director of the Royal BC Museum in Victoria and an Emily Carr expert par excellence. Along with Kathryn's corrections came suggestions for how to make a better, clearer point, and opened me to ideas I had not considered nor expected, which have made this book a better portrait not just of Woo but of Carr. Thank you, Kathryn.

Back when I was still bouncing the idea of a Woo biography off everyone I knew, my godfather William Luce took it as seriously as Jan Ross, and for much the same reason: because Emily Carr had loved Woo. A playwright famed for stage works in which such actors as Julie Harris and Christopher Plummer brought to life personalities of page and screen, in 2011 Bill visited the Royal BC Museum with me. He stood before Carr's paintings in awe, and as we looked in the museum shop for her books, he said, "Her life would make a wonderful play." (Julie Harris, who once visited the Emily Carr House in Victoria for the express purpose of finding out more about her, seems to have thought the same.) I agreed and hoped the books he bought would be translated into another of his dramas. They were not, but perhaps it was for the best. I remember, that day at the museum, how I ventured to say, "I'm actually thinking of writing a life of her monkey, Woo." Bill's eyes brightened, he took my arm and said, paraphrasing Emily Dickinson, "Now that's a book to lift your hat to!" Well, Bill, I did it. Thank you for teaching me how to write a life, and for teaching me how to live life too.

Without the magic of Story Book Farm Primate Sanctuary—the compassionate humans who manage it and the inspiring monkeys who are healing and learning to trust and learning how to be monkeys again there—none of the above would have come together. Thank you, Amy Cox Ferreira, Rachelle Hansen, Sarah Iannicello, Anita Kunz, Daina Liepa, Kim Meehan and Charmaine Quinn. And love to Bandit, Boo, Buddy, Cedric, Cheeko, Cody, Darwin, Gerdie, Julien, Keanu, Kizmet, Kye, Lexy, Mr. Jenkins, Pierre, Pockets, Pugsley, Remel and Rudy, and in memory of Sweet Pea (2001–2018) and George (1980?–2018). You are in good hands now.

Deepest gratitude to the following: John Adams, Eva Athanasiu (Art Gallery of Ontario), Lorna Crozier, Derek Fairbridge, Nicola Goshulak, Tim Gosley, Les Hayter, Allen Hirsch, Dr. Phyllis Marie Jensen, Allan Lannon, the late Ray Lewis, Joe Mabel, Randy Malamud, James Mayhew, Ronda Menzies, Sean William Menzies, Richard Natoli-Rombach, Ian Redmond, Linda Rogers, Nick Russell, Anny Scoones, Susan Short (National Gallery of Canada), Kelly-Ann Turkington (Royal BC Museum), Simone Vogel, Andrew Westoll and the staff of the City of Vancouver Archives.

And in thankful memory of my parents, who taught us from the cradle that animals are family too.

About Story Book Farm Primate Sanctuary

Story Book Farm Primate Sanctuary is a place of safety, offering freedom from fear, a place of healing and recovery from trauma. The sanctuary is home to nineteen monkeys from a variety of backgrounds, most with back-stories of exploitation and trauma.

Story Book Farm encourages friendships between the residents, as well as exploration and freedom of choice, restoring the ability to make decisions and control events that affect residents' lives.

Story Book Farm believes that all animals have rights; that animals have the right to live free of fear or pain from humans, in any form; and that we can all make a difference, one being at a time. Check out their website at: www.storybookmonkeys.org.

To donate: www.storybookmonkeys.org/donate.htm.

INDEX

Page numbers in **bold** refer to images in the photo insert.